DATE DUE

JUL 2 3 1990		
JAN 3 1 1993		
DEC 3 0 1997		

GAYLORD

PRINTED IN U.S.A.

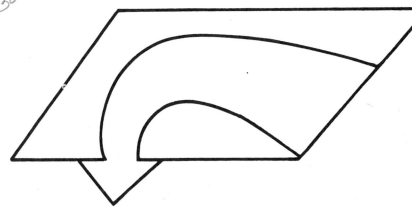

SHAPED CANVAS

By Bruce Bowman

 STERLING PUBLISHING CO., INC.   NEW YORK
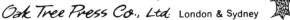 *Oak Tree Press Co., Ltd.* London & Sydney

I must extend my sincere appreciation to my students at Hale Junior High School, Woodland Hills, California, for allowing me to reproduce their paintings in this book. Special thanks to my wife, Julie, for her help in the photography and editing of the manuscript. Thanks also, to C. A. Mates for his editing assistance.

Copyright © 1976 by Sterling Publishing Co., Inc.
419 Park Avenue South, New York, N.Y. 10016
Distributed in Australia and New Zealand by Oak Tree Press Co., Ltd.,
P.O. Box J34, Brickfield Hill, Sydney 2000, N.S.W.
Distributed in the United Kingdom and elsewhere in the British Commonwealth
by Ward Lock Ltd., 116 Baker Street, London W 1
Manufactured in the United States of America

Library of Congress Catalog Card No.: 76-1183
Sterling ISBN 0-8069-5360-8 Trade   Oak Tree 7061-2173-2
5361-6 Library

Contents

Introduction

A SHAPED CANVAS is one that abandons the traditional square or rectangular form in favor of an outline that follows the angles and curves of the painted design. The design is carried over the sides to become the actual framing edge. The canvas is an essential part of the design, giving the artist many exciting possibilities not obtainable with the conventional painting surface. This phase of painting has not been explored by many artists, except for some of the painters associated with the Minimal and Pop Art movements. Images on shaped canvases are usually abstract, with a geometric pattern painted in a hard edge technique (edges that are sharp, with no shading or blending of colors). Occasionally a Pop Art image, such as a hot dog or ice cream cone, is used. In this case, the painting technique is realistic, with the contour of the canvas shaped to suit the image. It is precisely the physical contour of the canvas that makes the painting unique and dynamic, and provides much of its visual impact.

Because of its formed, irregular contours, a shaped canvas is as much a work of sculpture as it is a painting. Some artists have used deep supports to thrust massive paintings out from the supporting wall. These extreme-size works are almost part of the architecture. This unique art form is being used more and more in contemporary homes as an integral part of their interior design.

Shaped canvases can be constructed of various materials, but the most popular have been canvas over wood supports. Masonite with wood supports has also been used—even plastic and canvas over wire and steel. Because of the time-consuming construction, as well as structural complications, artists have often shied away from working

5

Illus. 1. Comic-book symbols are ideal subjects for shaped-canvas paintings.

with shaped canvases. Unfortunately, they have overlooked Styrofoam (a registered trade name of the Dow Chemical Co.)—a hard plastic-foam material that avoids all of these problems. Stretching canvas over Styrofoam is an easy, economical way to create a shaped canvas that cannot be distinguished from the traditional wood-supported structure. Besides its low cost, the advantages of Styrofoam are its light weight and its ease of handling. An artist using this material works with a knife and glue rather than saw and nails.

Painting the shaped canvas is a relatively simple procedure. Its hard-edge geometric forms are easily brushed on, especially the straight lines. These are obtained by placing masking tape on the painting surface, then removing it after two or three coats of quick-drying acrylics have been applied. Colors, which vary from bright and bold to soft pastel, reinforce the boldness of the forms. Glossy, matte, even metallic paint finishes can be used, heightening the dynamic effect of this unique painting surface.

Designing a Shaped Canvas

IN DESIGNING a shaped canvas, you can begin with a particular shape and sketch designs to suit its contour, or you can just start sketching designs and construct your canvas to fit the one you choose. In trying out ideas, it might be advisable to work on the contour and overall shape first. Sketch designs that relate to the form you have selected. If the results are unsatisfactory, switch to designing the internal forms. Many times this is the easier solution, for when you work out the internal design first, it will in most cases determine its own contours.

A shaped canvas does not need to be complicated or filled with intricate details to be interesting and visually exciting. A skillfully designed canvas is usually one that is well organized and this, in most cases, is simply a matter of basic composition. Ask yourself some questions about your design. Does it have variation? Are the sizes, shapes, colors, angles and curves different from each other (see Illus. 25 for an example)? Too much sameness creates a visual monotony. How do the forms within the shape work as a pattern? Do they flow together well and lead the viewer's eye around the canvas (see Illus. 35)? If they do not flow together, do they flow against each other? This opposition or contrast creates an internal conflict that can also be visually exciting. An excellent example of a harmonious as well as opposing flow of forms is the interlocking pattern in Illus. 52. To maintain a stability of the forms within your shaped canvas, it is important to achieve a visual balance. One way of doing this is to disperse the shapes and colors throughout the canvas and avoid concentrating them in one area.

7

Getting Ideas

Any painting starts with a series of rough ideas. From these you develop and polish the most promising design into the final work. Though time consuming, this process is the only way to be sure you get the best possible design out of the many alternatives. Professional designers and artists develop their ideas this way, and it is the best approach for students and beginners as well.

The first step is to get some ideas down on paper. Avoid trying to think of ideas in thought alone. They must be put down, for it is too easy to go from thinking of designs to random daydreaming. Also, when you develop the designs on paper, you can often see other possibilities and potential improvements. At this stage an eraser can be as much help as a pencil in developing your design. A 2-B pencil,

Illus. 2. Mechanical aids are useful in working out ideas for a canvas. Any rough sketch may be the springboard to a satisfying design.

a kneaded eraser for making changes, and some paper is all you need to get started.

Try freehand doodling to begin your series of rough sketches. This method often produces some of the most interesting effects. Besides, it is more fun than work, and can be more rewarding than racking your brains to come up with the ideal design. If this does not produce the desired results, try using some mechanical aids to facilitate the flow of ideas. A protractor, compass, French curves, templates, and triangles are all useful (see Illus. 2). Here again, start by experimenting and playing around with all sorts of possibilities. The clear plastic tools have the added advantage of allowing the partially completed designs to show through, letting you visualize the results before you actually draw additional lines.

Designing Suggestions

In developing a design, a good approach is to do as many different types of drawings as possible, trying not to get stuck on one particular style or line of thought. When you have completed a sufficient variety, look them over and see which ones look good (Illus. 3). If you are not satisfied with any of the images, try to analyze what is wrong and adjust your approach accordingly. When you find a particular design that meets with your approval, start concentrating on this specific shape or form. Change and modify it until you arrive at the final design for your canvas. Working in a more restricted sense narrows down the possibilities for a design.

In many cases, you may prefer a "Pop Art" image. A hamburger or an ice cream cone is the perfect shaped canvas for a child's, teenager's, or family room. Some other ideas that have been used by young artists are peace symbols, shooting stars and zap symbols. A salad bowl or piece of cake as a shaped canvas is ideal for a kitchen or breakfast area and flowers fit in anywhere. Having decided on a Pop Art subject, use photographs from magazines as a visual source for actually designing and painting the canvas. Most Pop paintings

Illus. 3. Here are four sheets of rough sketches, all suggesting possibilities for shaped canvases. You can see some of them developed into finished paintings in the color section of this book.

need to be quite realistic and it is easier to have a picture of the real thing at hand than to try guessing what it looks like.

With numerous designs completed and, hopefully, several acceptable ones, it is time to start working on the color scheme. Here too, it is advisable to have some alternates. When you start adding color, the design often changes and what looked good as a pencil sketch will be entirely different in color.

Selecting Colors

Color, because viewers respond to it more than any other element in art, is an important factor in designing a shaped canvas. The effect the colors are to have in the design should be determined at the

Illus. 4. Try turning your drawings, looking at them with the various sides at the top. The effect is sometimes surprisingly different.

Illus. 5. Use curved, flowing lines in your designs to create a feeling of motion.

beginning. Bold, striking colors demand attention. Subtle, soothing hues blend with an existing color motif. Pretty, appealing pastel shades are pleasing in themselves. All of them can be used to produce a visual effect. There are methods for obtaining whatever effect you prefer.

Values—the lightness and darkness of a color—are important because of the dramatic effect of the contrast of their extremes. Medium values or middle tones produce a muted image and are not as outstanding, but this may be desirable in some designs.

Color gives off a sensation of temperature. Red, yellow and orange produce a warm feeling, while blue, purple and green give a cooling effect. You might want to keep this in mind if you are planning your canvas for a particular room. Another significant function of color is the optical effect it creates. Warm colors tend to advance while cool

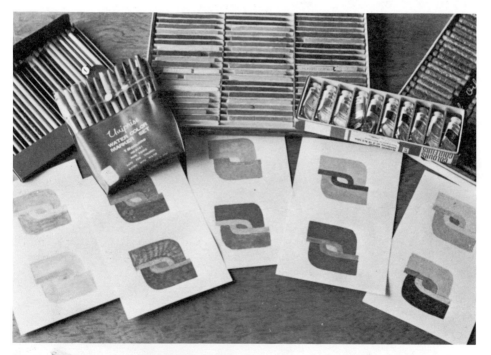

Illus. 6. Use colored pencils, soft-tip pens, chalk, gouache, pastels or other media to try out various color combinations.

Illus. 7. Mixing your own colors gives you an un-limited selection.

Illus. 8. Cut out swatches of the colors you mixed and try them in various combinations.

colors appear to recede. You might use this characteristic to make a small room appear larger or vice versa.

When it comes to actually selecting colors, the choice may be as simple as remembering a group of colors that you have seen together, like very much and want to use again. The usual process, however, is relating an unknown set of colors to the design. Start by determining the number of colors that you will need for the painting. Remember that it may be desirable to repeat some colors, particularly if there are many different areas to paint on the canvas. In working out the colors to be used on the canvas, you can use various media—soft-tip pens, transparent watercolors, gouache (opaque watercolors), chalk or oil, pastels, colored pencils, or even acrylic paints (Illus. 6). Any of these materials are available from art supply stores. A drawback to pencils, soft-tip pens, and pastels is that they do not mix completely, giving an uneven and inaccurate representation of the colors. If you have a large enough selection of colors in these media so that it is not necessary to mix them, it is an easy way to arrive at a choice of colors. With watercolor, gouache or acrylics, you have an unlimited number of color choices by mixing. A good way to work with these colors is to start mixing and make a quantity of small color swatches about one inch by one inch in size (Illus. 7). When they are dry, cut them out and arrange them in groups (Illus. 8). This method also works with paint manufacturers' color cards. After choosing the color grouping you prefer, the final step is always to paint in a small rough drawing of the design to see how the colors react together as a unit. This will give you a scaled-down idea of how the finished canvas will look. If it is not completely satisfactory, substitutions or another selection may be necessary.

When the design and color scheme of the shaped canvas is finalized, you are ready to start on the actual construction.

Constructing a Shaped Canvas

THE IDEAL MATERIAL to use as a base for the shaped canvas is Styrofoam, the hard foam-plastic material that is extraordinarily light and durable. It is fairly easy to crush so you must handle it with a reasonable amount of care. When it is covered with primed canvas,

Illus. 9. To make a base for a larger canvas, you may have to glue two or more sheets of Styrofoam together. Use extra strips on the back along the edges and to overlap the joint. Use weights to hold everything flat while the glue dries.

Illus. 10. Enlarge your selected sketch to a full-size
pattern.

Illus. 11. Cut out the
pattern as the first step in
transferring the outline to
the Styrofoam base.

however, its structure is reinforced, making it strong, while remaining light in weight. Styrofoam can be purchased in any crafts supply store and comes in sheets of various sizes up to 24 × 36 inches (60 × 90 cm.), in one- and two-inch (2.5- and 5-cm.) thicknesses. Anything smaller tends to lose its visual effectiveness. For larger canvases, you will have to glue two or more sheets together (Illus. 9). The 24 × 36-inch size is ideal, since one yard of primed canvas, which comes in 52-inch widths, will adequately cover the sheet.

Rather than trying to cut the sheet freehand, first sketch your design full-size on a sheet of paper, then transfer it to the Styrofoam

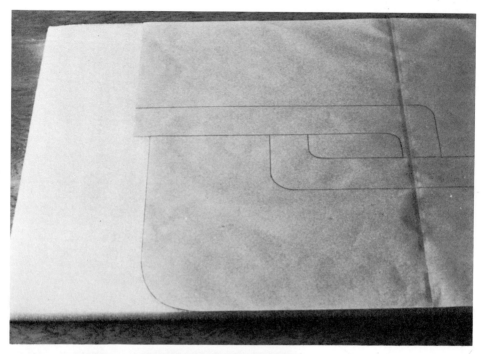

Illus. 12 (above). Lay the full-size outline pattern on top of the Styrofoam base.

Illus. 13. Trace around the outline with a pencil, being careful not to dig into the surface.

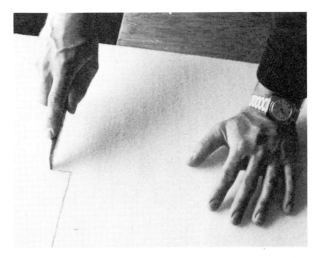

Illus. 14. Use light, even strokes with a sharp mat knife to cut out the Styrofoam base.

sheet. Use newsprint paper, wrapping paper or even newspaper for the pattern (Illus. 10). To enlarge a small sketch to a full-size pattern, divide both the sketch and the large paper into fourths. These serve as a reference grid, enabling you to work on one quarter at a time. You may have to do some erasing and redrawing until you get the pattern just right.

Cut out the full-size pattern and lay it in place on the Styrofoam sheet (Illus. 11 and 12). Use a pencil to sketch lightly around the

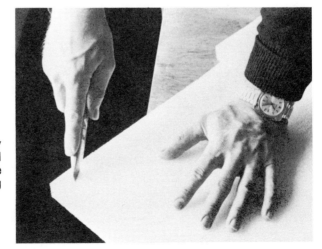

Illus. 15. Be especially careful near corners and edges not to crumble the material by forcing the blade.

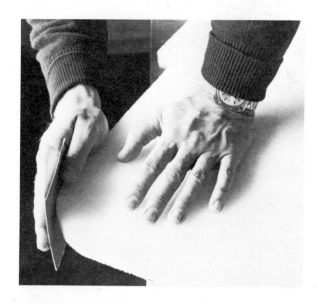

Illus. 16. Smooth off any rough edges by sanding them lightly with fine-grade sandpaper.

Illus. 17. Here is a finished, shaped-Styrofoam base.

Illus. 18. Place the prepared base face down against the back of a piece of primed canvas and make a pencil outline around the edge.

shape, trying to avoid digging into the foam (Illus. 13). Be sure to hold the knife straight up to ensure a sharp 90-degree edge. Use light, even strokes with a sharp mat knife to cut out the shape (Illus. 14 and 15). Repeat the cuts, going a little deeper each time. With a one-inch-thick piece of Styrofoam, plan to go over each single line at least five times. Avoid any sawing motions or forcing the blade, or you will crumble or smash the edges. You can correct edges that are slightly crumbled or lumpy by sanding them lightly with fine-grade sand-paper, using long, light, even strokes (Illus. 16).

Place the cut-out Styrofoam shape against the back of the primed canvas (primed side facing downwards). Next, make a pencil outline of the Styrofoam form on the back of the canvas (Illus. 18). Take away the Styrofoam and add a 2- to 3-inch outline (5- to 7.5-cm.) around the pencilled shape. This is the portion that will wrap around

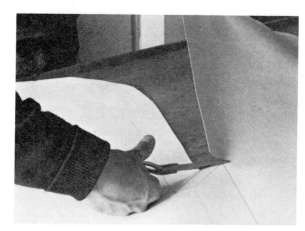

Illus. 19. After adding 2 or 3 inches (5 or 7.5 cm.) to the outline, trim away the excess canvas.

Illus. 20. Cut flaps at the corners and towards the middle of curves to keep the canvas from buckling when you pin it down.

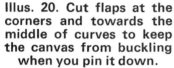

the edges to be glued and pinned to the back. With a pair of scissors, trim off the excess canvas (Illus. 19). To prevent the edges of the canvas from buckling on the curves when you pin it down, cut the curved portions in strips that angle towards the middle of the curve (Illus. 20). Sharp curves call for more strips or flaps than gradual curves. Sharp V's or 90-degree corners will likely produce gaps that let the Styrofoam show through. You can hide this easily by inserting a strip of canvas as wide as the thickness of the Styrofoam edge behind the flaps. Use white glue to fasten the strip to the edge of the Styrofoam, holding everything in place with masking tape until the glue dries. The touched-up gap will be hardly noticeable.

Illus. 21 (above). Note the large number of flaps necessary for a shape with several curves.

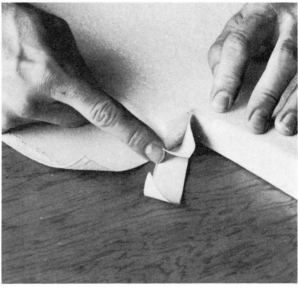

Illus. 22. An extra strip of canvas attached to the edge of the base will prevent it from showing through any gaps between the flaps.

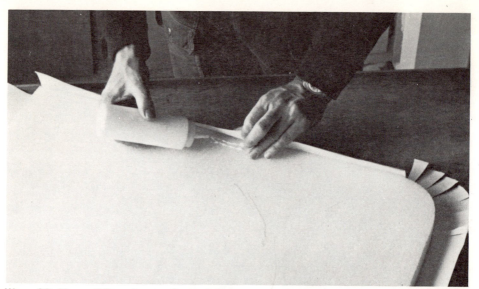

Illus. 23. Use white glue to fasten the canvas to the back of the Styrofoam base.

Illus. 24. With dressmaker's pins, fasten a few inches at the middle of one side, then switch to the opposite side of the frame.

Illus. 25. In this abstract cloud picture, the contrasting inner shapes echo the framing edge in an interesting pattern.

Illus. 26. This bolt of psychedelic lightning is borrowed from comic-book art.

Illus. 27. On this shaped canvas a fireworks of swirling
flowers emerges from a pot.

Illus. 28. Interlocking, geometric fans of color make an appealing design.

Illus. 29. These elegant swerves of color produce a graceful canvas.

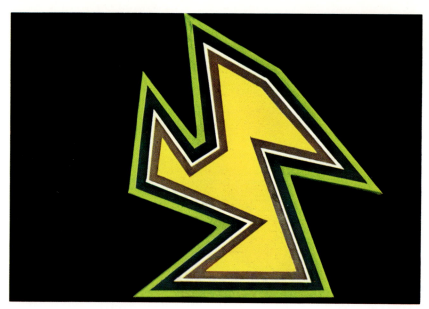

Illus. 30. In choosing colors for your canvas, consider the background against which it will be hung.

Illus. 31. A black wall greatly enhances this man-in-the-moon
canvas.

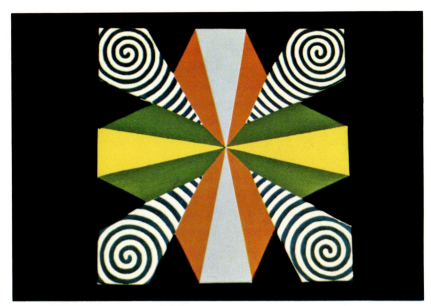

Illus. 32. These converging angles draw the eye quickly to the middle of the design.

Illus. 33. In this design, the overlapping triangles provide stability for the whirlpools of color.

Illus. 34. These quarter circles point and angle in different directions.

Illus. 35. Contrasting warm and cool colors add to this intriguing pattern of interlocking circles.

Illus. 36 and 37. The series of concentric shapes seems to recede into the canvas in the design at the left, but springs out from the middle in the design at the right. Do your eyes see them this way?

Illus. 38 and 39. The round canvas at left is divided across the middle, with a different sequence of circles in each half in opposition to one another. The two halves of the canvas at the right mirror one another and seem to overlap.

Illus. 40. The internal design of this painting is framed by the contours of the canvas itself.

Illus. 41. The round, soft, curved forms of the central design are in marked contrast to the field of bold, hard, straight lines.

Illus. 42. You can use shaped canvases for representational paintings as well as abstracts. They are more fun when you choose unconventional subjects.

Illus. 43. Soft pastel colors are as effective in their way as brighter bolder colors.

Illus. 44. Here is a rainbow of colors for the top of a staircase.

Illus. 45. These shooting stars leave a trail of color.

Illus. 46. Note the difference in appearance of the same canvas hung against a different background.

Illus. 47. The shape of the canvas itself suggests a butterfly more than the painted-on colors.

Illus. 48. The richness of the colors makes this an outstanding work.

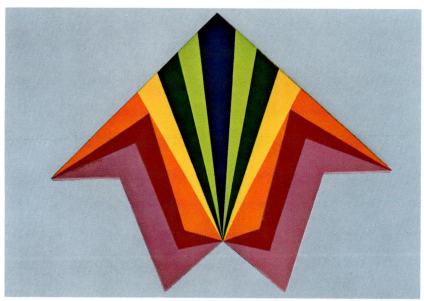

Illus. 49. The arrangement of the interior color patterns do not relate to the penguin shape at all, yet flow together harmoniously.

Illus. 50. This canvas shows a white dove emerging from cool clouds into a warm rainbow of color.

Illus. 51. Note the effect of displaying the same canvas against a different background.

Illus. 52. In this composition the dark shapes dominate the others and direct the eyes' movement around the canvas.

Illus. 53. This abstract design immediately brings to mind a flag flying in a breeze.

Illus. 54. This canvas is based on the opposition of direction as well as the warm and cool colors.

Illus. 55. The value gradation of the stripes dramatizes the richness of the colors of this canvas.

Illus. 56. The canvas and the brick wall each enhance the other in
this case.

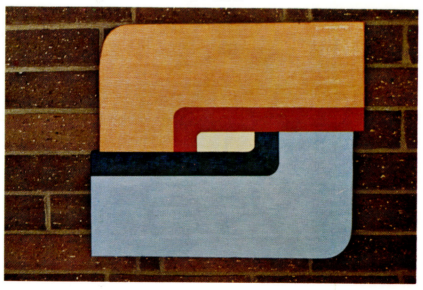

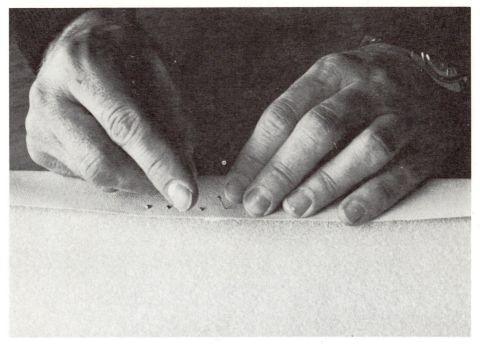

Illus. 57. Push the pins in at a slight angle towards the edges so they will not pull out as you stretch the canvas.

In the actual stretching of the canvas over the Styrofoam form, follow the same method you would use on rectangular stretcher bars. Start by fastening a couple of inches at the middle of one side, then switch to the middle of the opposite side of the frame. Turn the work 90 degrees and fasten the middle section of each end. Following the same sequence, keep going until you reach the corners of the frame. Working in this manner instead of completely doing one side at a time reduces the chances of ending up with wrinkles in the corners, or of warping the form.

Fastening the canvas to the Styrofoam is a simple procedure. First apply white glue and insert a few dressmaker's pins (Illus. 23). Apply the glue liberally since the pores of the foam will absorb some of it. The pins should go in at a slight angle with their points headed towards the edge so they will not pull out in the stretching (Illus. 57).

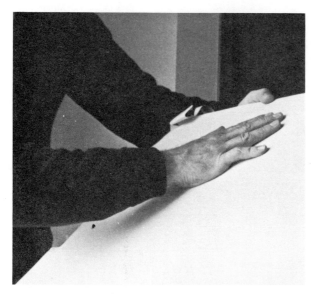

Illus. 58. Smooth any slack out of the canvas by running the flat of your hand over it, moving towards the area to be pinned.

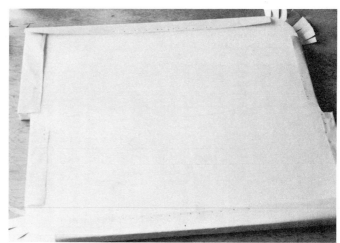

Illus. 59. Save the corners for the last.

When you switch from one side to another, run the flat of your hand over the canvas, smoothing it towards the area to be pinned. Form the canvas over the edge, pulling it tight enough to take up the slack on the surface (Illus. 58). Do not pull the canvas too hard over the back or you will crush and round the sharp square edges. If the form

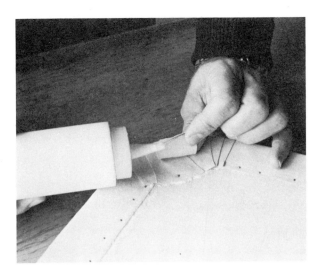

Illus. 60. Overlap the flaps as you glue and pin the corners.

Illus. 61. A properly worked corner has all of the flaps lying flat against the edge of the base.

being shaped has many curves and/or angles, there will be quite a few areas with edges overlapping the sides (Illus. 61). These are not so noticeable after the canvas is painted, provided the angles are slight and there are not too many of them. With too many curves, the flaps will be obvious but you can cover them easily with a strip of canvas

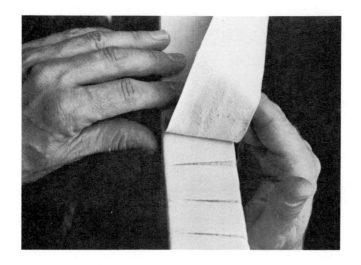

Illus. 62. As a final
touch, you can glue
a strip of canvas
around the edge to
cover up the flaps.

as wide as the edge. Simply glue the strip around the edges and tape
it down until it dries (Illus. 62).

It is not necessary to remove the pins from the back of the canvas
when the glue has dried. Avoid putting any pins in the sides of the
foam. Use masking tape instead.

If the canvas surface is loose or slightly wrinkled after the glued
tabs are dry, go over it lightly with a slightly moist towel or rag. Wipe
the surface off immediately and let the canvas dry for about an hour.

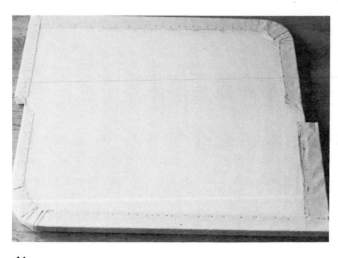

Illus. 63. Here is the
back of a
completed canvas.

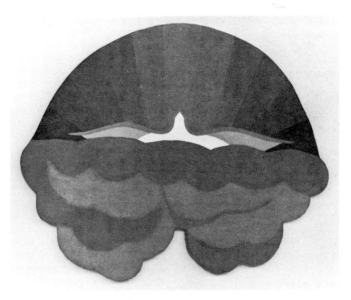

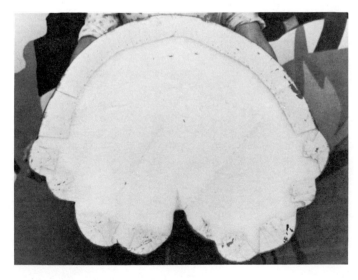

Illus. 65. Back view
of the same canvas.

This will shrink the canvas somewhat, taking up a small amount of slack. Repeat the procedure if the surface is still loose, but you must avoid putting too much moisture on the surface at any one time since it will buckle and warp the shaped canvas.

Illus. 66. This abstract butterfly is shown in full color on page 36.

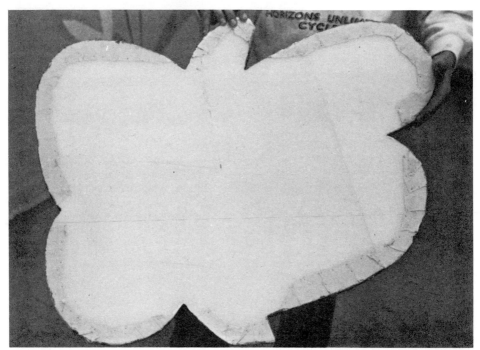

Illus. 67. Note how pieces of hard plastic foam were joined together to make a large enough base for this canvas.

Other Shaped Canvases

Masonite

An alternative method for constructing a shaped canvas is to glue and clamp 2 × 3-inch (5 × 7.5-cm.) white pine to a piece of Masonite cut to the proper contour (Illus. 68). Notice how the curve is cut and shaped. Before painting on the design, coat the form with gesso to seal the surface. Without the protective coating of gesso, numerous coats of paint would be required due to the absorption of the Masonite surface. Though extremely sturdy, Masonite forms are quite heavy.

Illus. 68. Canvases made of Masonite fastened to a wooden frame are quite sturdy. You must coat the Masonite with gesso before starting to paint, however, to prevent it from absorbing your paint.

Canvas Over Wood Stretcher Bars

This is the conventional method of making forms for shaped canvases. Plywood triangles are nailed and glued in the corners for stability (Illus. 69). The triangles are placed below the surface of the bars so the painted edges will fit flatly against the wall when the canvas is hung. Alternatively, you can use wooden struts or braces nailed and glued diagonally in the corners instead. This is a matter of your own preference, but some form of support is needed or the frame will warp when it is stretched, and hang lopsided on the wall.

Illus. 69. The braces are fastened to the back side of the wood stretcher bars so they do not interfere with the canvas.

Illus. 70. Stretch the canvas over the frame, fastening it at the middle of each side first, then working outward to the corners.

Lighter weight redwood was used for the frame in Illus. 69 instead of the popular white pine. The inside edge of the frame is bevelled down $\frac{1}{4}$ inch below the outer edge. Otherwise it may show up as a line on the canvas after it has been painted.

The shaped canvas in Illus. 70 was not too complicated to construct since the shaping was slight, but it is still a more involved process than making canvas with a Styrofoam support. A more complex shaped canvas on a wood frame would involve a great deal of planning and construction time.

Painting the Shaped Canvas

To AVOID ERASURES and corrections on the painting surface, draw the design out first on the large sheet of paper you originally used as a pattern for cutting the Styrofoam. Darken the back of the sheet with the side of a soft (2B) pencil to make it act like a carbon, then trace

Illus. 71. In preparation for transferring your design to the canvas, darken the back of the pattern with a soft pencil. You can see more clearly where the lines are by holding the paper against a window.

Illus. 72. With your pattern over the canvas, trace over the lines with a ball-point pen. Use a straightedge on long lines.

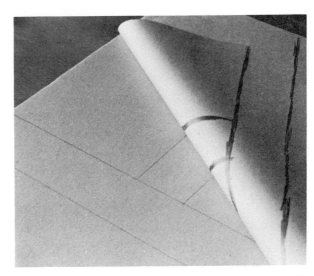

Illus. 73. With the design transferred, you are ready to begin painting.

Illus. 74. Acrylic paints are ideal for shaped canvases. They dry quickly, are easy to clean up, and they come in a wide range of rich colors.

it onto the canvas. You need only darken the areas behind the lines to be traced. To see more clearly where these lines are, hold the paper against a window (Illus. 71). Position the darkened paper over the stretched canvas, using masking tape to hold it in place. Draw over the lines with a ball-point pen, using only enough pressure to have the lines trace off onto the canvas surface (Illus. 73). Use a straightedge on long lines to keep them true (Illus. 72).

With the design traced on the canvas, you are ready to start painting. Oils can be used, but acrylics are much more practical, due to their short drying time. Nylon brushes spread acrylics easier and the bristles do not absorb too much water, which can become a problem later on. You can clean your brushes simply by working a little liquid soap into the bristles and rinsing them well in water.

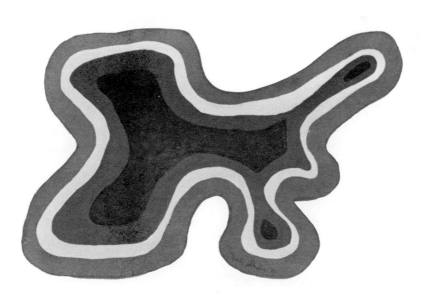

Illus. 75. Use masking tape to paint canvases like the one at top with long straight lines. Canvases with many curves have to be painted freehand.

Illus. 76. Use strips of masking tape to keep long lines straight. The tape also allows the paint to build up, leaving a sharp edge when it is removed.

Acrylics start to harden and thicken up after a short time, but you can keep the paint in workable condition indefinitely by spraying a fine mist of water over the surface from time to time. Keep a spray bottle handy for this purpose.

Have your rough sketch at hand, showing the colors you have selected. The problem now is to duplicate or match the colors in the rough. Avoid using paints straight from the tube unless you particularly want these intense, standard colors (Illus. 74). To obtain rich colors, mix the paints. To tint or lighten your colors, add white. To shade or darken them, add black. If you need to tone down, neutralize or grey any of your colors, mix a little of that color's complementary color with it.

To gain variety in your color range, work with analogous colors, those in between the primary and secondary colors. For example, instead of using orange straight from the tube, mix a little red or yellow with it. The result is an intermediate red-orange or yellow-orange. Better yet, you might try mixing orange completely from red and yellow. The ability to mix and match colors well comes from experiment and practice. The objective is to get away from relying only on pre-mixed colors; your paintings will be more interesting and will look more professional for the effort.

When starting, mix a large batch of paint, enough for three or four coats if they are needed. Keep the paint moist by placing it in a cup with a sheet of plastic wrap over the top. Save a little of each color for a final touch-up. This will save you from the problem of more mixing and color matching.

Illus. 77. Apply tape wherever you can but be sure it is pressed down tight as the least gap will allow paint to seep under and blur the outline of the painted areas.

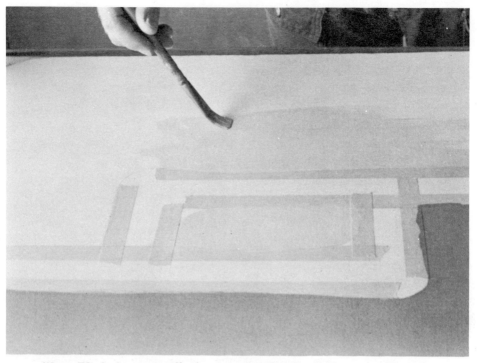

Illus. 78. It is generally best to apply the lighter colors first.

When applying the paint to the canvas it is best to paint the lighter colors first since they are easier to cover up. Two coats of paint are usually sufficient, but certain slightly transparent colors, such as yellow and orange, may require three coats, possibly four. Your goal is consistency of color without streaks or mottling. Several thin coats will assure the evenness of your colors.

Lay down strips of masking tape to keep straight lines from wavering (Illus. 76). Run your thumbnail over the edge to be painted to be sure the tape is pressed down tightly. The least gap will allow paint to seep under the tape and blur the edges of the painted areas.

Apply tape wherever you can. When an area has been thoroughly coated, pull up the tape and reapply it so that the next unpainted areas

Illus. 79. Once the paint has hardened, peel the tape away carefully.

Illus. 80. Be sure that painted areas are dry before you apply tape over them.

57

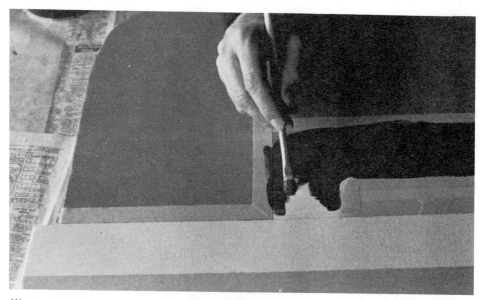

Illus. 81. When you are painting curves or along short lines, work freehand with a small brush.

Illus. 82. Allow a filled-in area to dry before removing the masking tape.

Illus. 83. Masking tape peels right off the previously painted area, leaving a sharp clear line at the edge.

Illus. 84. When all of the areas have been painted and the last tape removed, touch up by hand any blurry sections of line. See the finished canvas in color on page 40.

Illus. 85. Acrylic paints cover well, are easy to use, and are easy to clean up.

can be covered (Illus. 79 and 80). In many instances you will have to apply tape over already-painted areas. Be sure these are completely dry before sticking on the tape. To speed up drying, you can put your canvas in a sunlit area, but keep it indoors so that particles blowing in the wind do not stick in the wet surface.

When painting curves, forget the masking tape and do them by hand. You may need a smaller brush and a few attempts to get smooth, even curves, but you can do it with a little patience. Slowly paint out the bumps and blurs in small, even strokes, covering a little bit at a time (Illus. 84). Be sure to carry all of the lines and curves over the edges and down the sides of the shaped canvas. This is what gives the shaped canvas much of its dynamic, three-dimensional quality.

Illus. 86. The final touches are important to the appearance of the finished work. Note how the design is carried around over the edges onto the sides of the canvas.

Illus. 87. You should also touch up any areas where the paint is too thin.

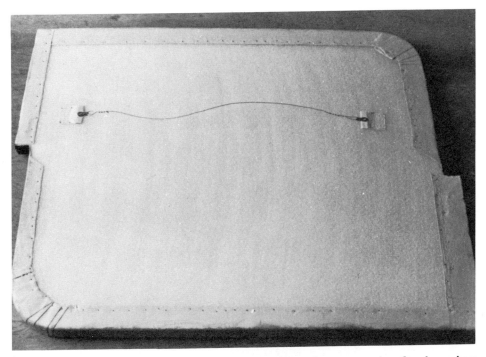

Illus. 88. This back view of a painted canvas shows a wire for hanging held in place by two cloth-backed hooks.

To hang your shaped canvas, glue and pin two cloth-backed hooks to the Styrofoam back and connect them with a wire (Illus. 88).

The process of creating a shaped canvas is relatively simple, but once completed it is a unique and interesting new dimension in almost any interior setting. The pleasure and admiration shown by those who view it will surely be encouragement for you to produce many more.

Index

Robert Charles Wilson

Robert Charles Wilson

JULIAN*

*A Christmas Story

Introduction by Robert J. Sawyer

PS PUBLISHING 2006

Published in November 2006 by PS Publishing Ltd by
arrangement with the author. All rights reserved by the author.

FIRST EDITION

ISBN
Hardcover: 1–905834–27–6
Paperback: 1–905834–26–8

Printed and bound in Great Britain by
Biddles Ltd., King's Lynn, Norfolk

PS Publishing Ltd
Grosvenor House
1 New Road
Hornsea, HU18 1PG
England

E-mail: editor@pspublishing.co.uk

Visit our website at **www.pspublishing.co.uk**.

ROBERT CHARLES WILSON:
EIGHT RANDOM THOUGHTS

by Robert J. Sawyer

ROBERT CHARLES WILSON was the Author Guest of Honor at Ad Astra, Toronto's annual science-fiction convention, in 2003. As the con was approaching, Bob confessed to his wife, the vivacious Sharry, that he had no idea how to craft a Guest of Honor speech. She said, "Just write down the next six or eight thoughts that come into your head—give them five minutes each, and you're done." Bob took her advice and gave the best GoH talk I've ever heard (it's online as "Eight Random Thoughts" at the indispensable *Made in Canada* site celebrating Canadian SF: *geocities.com/canadian_sf*).

Well, in a spirit of homage—and because I have no better idea of how to capture all the complexity and wonder that is the man in question—I hereby offer up eight random thoughts on Robert Charles Wilson.

1. He's an excellent writer.

Not just an excellent science-fiction writer—which is sometimes said when one wants to damn with faint praise—but an excellent writer, period. He's one of those, like Theodore Sturgeon (to whom Bob was often compared early on), whom we can hold up as incontestable proof that SF does produce writing as fine as anything in the mainstream. I say Bob used to be compared to Sturgeon; he's still every bit as good, but Bob's focus has shifted, quite noticeably of late, to hard SF, with novels such as *Blind Lake* and *Spin*—which does make for a problem: there is in fact no one to compare the modern Bob Wilson to. He's *sui generis:* a hard-SF writer with the soul of a poet; a dreamer who can write with equal facility about cosmic events spanning billions of years and single heartbreaking moments in quiet, ordinary lives.

2. Bob's writing is fractal.

Many authors shine best at a specific length, but Bob Wilson's work shows the same marvelous qualities at any scale. He's had a pair of extraordinary thousand-word microfictions published in the British science journal *Nature* (one of which was subsequently picked up for Gardner Dozois's *Year's Best* anthology). He's written stunning short stories of more traditional lengths (many of which are collected in *The Perseids*). His novelette "The Cartesian Theater" has been singled out by multiple reviewers as the best piece in the remarkable 2006 anthology *Future Shocks*, edited by Lou Anders, and "Julian: A Christmas Story," the novella you're about to read, is a masterwork. As for novels, Bob serves 'em up both short and long: *Bios* can't be more than 60,000 words, while *Spin* weighs in at 140,000 (and he's not done yet—for the first time ever, Bob is writing a sequel; yes, folks, the Spin Cycle has begun!). But no matter what length he's working at, Bob provides pitch-perfect, highly polished prose; brilliant, original speculations (I'm frankly jealous of the genius behind the central conceits in *The Chronoliths, Blind Lake,* and *Spin*); and characters so nuanced and vivid you'll swear you can hear them gently breathing if you hold one of his books up to your ear.

3. Bob loves science fiction.

I mean, he *really* loves it. How can I tell? Well, there's a science-fiction bookstore near Bob's home called Sci-Fi World—and that's where he chose to get married. Actually, he and Sharry tied the knot in the Sci-Fi Café, a fast-food joint attached to the store; the signature item on the menu is the twelve-ounce Mothership Burger. It turned out to be a superlative venue for the wedding of a guy who loves to read SF, loves to write it, and loves to talk, as he often does with great affection, about what he calls the genre's wonderful, weird, gaudy history. (Bob has done a great job of educating Sharry about this crazy stuff he loves so much; Sharry, incidentally, is a proofreader for Harlequin romances—theirs is an inspiring cross-ghetto union.)

4. Bob hates science fiction.

Or, more precisely, he hates what's wrong with the field—and he knows exactly what that is. In the summer of 2005, Bob, Nalo Hopkinson, and I were summoned down to the Canadian Broadcasting Corporation's studios to record a joint interview for a radio documentary about SF. During it, Bob made a point that I'm still repeating (with attribution!) about SF having become so inbred, and so reliant on assumed familiarity with its core texts, that it has set up an insurmountable barrier to newcomers. But Bob's own work is an antidote for that. He writes for a larger audience; although his concepts are as mind-blowing as anything in Robert Forward or Larry Niven, anyone can read and enjoy a Bob Wilson book (indeed, my own father reads only two SF authors: me, out of paternal pride, and Bob).

5. Bob's an outsider.

And he likes it that way, I think. The dust jacket for the gorgeous hardcover of his latest novel, *Spin*, says he lives in Toronto, but that's not true. The northern border of Toronto is a street called Steeles Avenue, and he lives just beyond that. I think this is wonderfully appropriate: Bob is just outside of a lot of things. He was born in the US, but now lives in Canada, looking back at his homeland from just beyond its borders—a circumstance clearly echoed in his writing: *Blind Lake* is all about eavesdropping from a distance; *Spin* puts a literal, physical border around Earth, and has a Martian look on. (Yes, a Martian in modern SF—and he pulls it off!) Speaking of Mars, I remember the absolute glee with which Bob watched every day as new images taken by *Spirit* and *Opportunity* were beamed back from there; Bob was in his heaven, comfortable in his bright, airy home, old vinyl records playing on the tube-driven stereos he lovingly restores, peeking in at the goings-on on an alien world . . .

6. He's won lots of awards.

And, I'm proud to say, I helped give him his first. Long before Bob and I became friends, I was on the jury for the Philip K. Dick Award, which honors the year's best SF book published in the US in paperback. The other jurors and I kept grousing that most of what we'd seen was unworthy, and, in one of our conference calls for deliberating, I said, "You know, I just read a book that was better than anything that's been submitted—*Mysterium*, by this guy, Robert Charles Wilson." Another juror piped up to say he'd admired *Mysterium*, too; we got on to Bantam and had them send copies to the rest of the jury, and Bob was ultimately named our winner. Since then, he's won the John W. Campbell Memorial Award (for *The Chronoliths*), and three Canadian Aurora Awards (for the short story "The Perseids" and the novels *Darwinia* and *Blind Lake*), plus he's been nominated for four Hugos, three World Fantasy Awards, and two Nebulas, and had three of his titles named Notable Books of the Year by the *New York Times*. It's a CV better than that of 99% of the writers the SF field has ever produced, but, in a field plagued by giant egos, he never mentions any of this. Our man Bob does no self-promotion, rarely goes to cons, doesn't have a blog, doesn't maintain a website. He just writes, and lets his brilliant words speak for themselves.

7. He's unassuming.

You might think a guy who uses three names would be swaggering and pompous—the Charles Foster Kane of sci-fi; alternatively, you could be waiting for *Locus* to report that he's been arrested as a serial killer, SF's own John Wayne Gacy. But, in fact, Bob's triple-decker moniker is to distinguish him from Robert Anton Wilson (although these days, I suspect it's the *Illuminati* author who is less well known); there already were authors using "Robert Wilson" and "Robert C. Wilson." But you've got to give Bob credit; he really did try not to have such an overwhelming byline: his first published story, in *Analog*, way back in 1975, was signed Bob Chuck Wilson. (On the other hand, the less said about Bob's occasional pseudonym Uriah Cuthbert Poon the better . . .)

8. He's my brother.

See, in SF circles, we're known as "Rob and Bob," or—as I've overheard it said a couple of times (and I'm sure Bob cringes as much as I do at this)—the Bobbsey Twins: two middle-aged, balding, bearded, bespectacled science-fiction writers living in Toronto. We've also been called (by the *Ottawa Citizen*, no less) "the Martin and Lewis of SF." But I think the comparison is more like Kirk and Spock: I'm outgoing; Bob's reserved. I'm constantly joking around; Bob's wit is subtle and dry. And yet, as Kirk once observed, he and Spock are brothers (to which Bob might reply, as Spock did on that occasion, that, "Rob is speaking somewhat figuratively, and with undue emotion, but what he says is logical and I do, in fact, agree with it." Of course, we weren't *born* brothers, but we became so—and I know precisely when. In 1998 Tor Books, and Tor's Canadian distributor, H.B. Fenn and Company, sent Bob and me out on book tour together, promoting his *Darwinia* and my *Factoring Humanity*. We hardly knew each other then, and we were both somewhat nervous, I think—after all, spending many sleep-deprived days together on the road was a recipe for friction. But there was none; instead, Bob and I bonded, becoming the very best of friends. Tor and Fenn teamed us up again in 2005, sending us to fourteen cities in fourteen days promoting my *Mindscan* and his *Spin*; every moment was a joy. There really is no one I feel closer to in this profession, nor anyone I like more. That I happen to think he's also just about the best writer in the business is merely a bonus. But don't take my word for it—turn the page and see for yourself.

Robert J. Sawyer
August, 2006

JULIAN*

* A Christmas Story

1

THIS IS A STORY about Julian Comstock, better known as Julian the Agnostic or (after his uncle) Julian Conqueror. But it is not about his conquests, such as they were, or his betrayals, or about the War in Labrador, or Julian's quarrels with the Church of the Dominion. I witnessed many of those events—and will no doubt write about them, ultimately—but this narrative concerns Julian when he was young, and I was young, and neither of us was famous.

2

IN LATE OCTOBER OF 2172—an election year—Julian and I,
along with his mentor Sam Godwin, rode to the Tip east of the
town of Williams Ford, where I came to possess a book, and
Julian tutored me in one of his heresies.

It was a brisk, sunny day. There was a certain resolute prompt-
ness to the seasons in that part of Athabaska, in those days.
Our summers were long, languid, and hot. Spring and fall were
brief, mere custodial functions between the extremes of weather.
Winters were short but biting. Snow set in around the end of
December, and the River Pine generally thawed by late March.

Today might be the best we would get of autumn. It was a
day we should have spent under Sam Godwin's tutelage, perhaps sparring, or target-shooting, or reading chapters from the
Dominion History of the Union. But Sam was not a heartless
overseer, and the kindness of the weather had suggested the possibility of an Outing, and so we had gone to the stables, where my
father worked, and drawn horses, and ridden out of the Estate
with lunches of black bread and salt ham in our back-satchels.

We rode east, away from the hills and the town. Julian and I
rode ahead; Sam rode behind, a watchful presence, his Pittsburgh
rifle ready in the saddle holster at his side. There was no immediate

threat of trouble, but Sam Godwin believed in perpetual preparedness; if he had a gospel, it was BE PREPARED; also, SHOOT FIRST; and probably, DAMN THE CONSEQUENCES. Sam, who was old (nearly fifty), wore a dense brown beard stippled with wiry white hairs, and was dressed in what remained presentable of his tan-and-green Army of the Californias uniform, and a cloak to keep the wind off. He was like a father to Julian, Julian's own true father having performed a gallows dance some years before. Lately he had been more vigilant than ever, for reasons he had not discussed, at least with me.

Julian was my age (seventeen), and we were approximately the same height, but there the resemblance ended. Julian had been born an aristo; my family was of the leasing class. His skin was clear and pale where mine was dark and lunar. (I was marked by the same Pox that took my sister Flaxie to her grave in '63.) His hair was long and almost femininely clean; mine was black and wiry, cut to stubble by my mother with her sewing scissors, and I washed it once a week or so—more often in summer, when the brook behind the cottage ran clean and cool. His clothes were linen and, in places, silk, brass-buttoned, cut to fit; my shirt and pants were coarse hempen cloth, sewn to a good approximation but obviously not the work of a New York tailor.

And yet we were friends, and had been friends for three years, since we met by chance in the forested hills west of the Duncan and Crowley Estate, where we had gone to hunt, Julian with his fine Porter & Earle cassette rifle and me with a simple muzzle-loader. We both loved books, especially the boys' books written in those days by an author named Charles Curtis

Easton.* I had been carrying a copy of Easton's *Against the Brazilians*, illicitly borrowed from the Estate library; Julian had recognized the title, but refrained from ratting on me, since he loved the book as much as I did and longed to discuss it with a fellow enthusiast (of which there were precious few among his aristo relations)—in short, he did me an unbegged favor, and we became fast friends despite our differences.

In those early days I had not known how fond he was of blasphemy. But I had learned since, and it had not deterred me. Much.

We had not set out with the specific aim of visiting the Tip; but at the nearest crossroad Julian turned west, riding past cornfields and gourdfields already harvested and sun-whitened split-rail fences on which dense blackberry gnarls had grown up. The air was cool but the sun was fiercely bright. Julian and Sam wore broad-brimmed hats to protect their faces; I wore a plain linen pakool hat, sweat-stained, rolled about my ears. Before long we passed the last rude shacks of the indentured laborers, whose near-naked children gawked at us from the roadside, and it became obvious we were going to the Tip, because where else on this road was there to go?—unless we continued east for many hours, all the way to the ruins of the old towns, from the days of the False Tribulation.

The Tip was located far from Williams Ford to prevent poaching and disorder. There was a strict pecking order to the

---

* Whom I would meet when he was sixty years old, and I was a newcomer to the book trade—but that's another story.

7

Tip. This is how it worked: professional scavengers hired by the Estate brought their pickings from the ruined places to the Tip, which was a pine-fenced enclosure (a sort of stockade) in a patch of grassland and prairie flowers. There the newly-arrived goods were roughly sorted, and riders were dispatched to the Estate to make the high-born aware of the latest acquisitions, and various aristos (or their trusted servants) would ride out to claim the prime gleanings. The next day, the leasing class would be allowed to sort through what was left; after that, if anything remained, indentured laborers could rummage among it, if they calculated it worthwhile to make the journey.

Every prosperous town had a Tip; though in the east it was sometimes called a Till, a Dump, or an Eebay.

Today we were fortunate: several wagonloads of scrounge had lately arrived, and riders had not yet been sent to notify the Estate. The gate was manned by a Home Guard, who looked at us suspiciously until Sam announced the name of Julian Comstock; then the guard briskly stepped aside, and we went inside the enclosure.

Many of the wagons were still unloading, and a chubby Tipman, eager to show off his bounty, hurried toward us as we dismounted and moored our horses. "Happy coincidence!" he cried. "Gentlemen!" Addressing mostly Sam by this remark, with a cautious smile for Julian and a disdainful sidelong glance at me. "Anything *in particular* you're looking for?"

"Books," Julian said promptly, before Sam or I could answer.

"Books! Ordinarily, I set aside books for the Dominion Conservator . . ."

"The boy is a Comstock," Sam said. "I don't suppose you mean to balk him."

The Tipman reddened. "No, not at all . . . in fact we came across something in our digging . . . a sort of *library in miniature* . . . I'll show you, if you like."

This was intriguing, especially to Julian, who beamed as if he had been invited to a Christmas party. We followed the stout Tipman to a freshly-arrived canvasback wagon, from which a laborer was tossing bundled piles into a stack beside a tent.

These twine-wrapped bales were books . . . old, tattered, and wholly free of the Dominion Stamp of Approval. They must have been more than a century old; for although they were faded they had obviously once been colorful and expensively printed, not made of stiff brown paper like the Charles Curtis Easton books of modern times. They had not even rotted much. Their smell, under the cleansing Athabaska sunlight, was inoffensive.

"Sam!" Julian whispered. He had already drawn his knife and was slicing through the twine.

"Calm down," suggested Sam, who was not an enthusiast like Julian.

"Oh, but—*Sam!* We should have brought a cart!"

"We can't carry away armloads, Julian, nor would we ever have been allowed to. The Dominion scholars will have all this. Though perhaps you can get away with a volume or two."

The Tipman said, "These are from Lundsford." Lundsford was the name of a ruined town thirty or so miles to the southeast. The Tipman leaned toward Sam Godwin, who was his own age, and said: "We thought Lundsford had been mined out a decade ago. But even a dry well may freshen. One of my workers spotted a low place off the main excavations—a sort of *sink-hole*: the recent rain had cut it through. Once a basement or warehouse of some kind. Oh, sir, we found good china there, and glasswork, and many more books than this . . . most were mildewed, but some had been protected under a kind of stiff oilcloth, and were lodged beneath a partially-collapsed ceiling . . . there had been a fire, but they survived it . . ."

"Good work, Tipman," Sam Godwin said.

"Thank you, sir! Perhaps you could remember me to the great men of the Estate?" And he gave his name (which I have forgotten).

Julian had fallen to his knees amidst the compacted clay and rubble of the Tip, lifting up each book in turn and examining it with wide eyes. I joined him in his exploration.

I had never much liked the Tip. It had always seemed to me a haunted place. And of course it *was* haunted: that was its purpose, to house the revenants of the past, ghosts of the False Tribulation startled out of their century-long slumber. Here was evidence of the best and worst of the people who had inhabited the Years of Vice and Profligacy. Their fine things were very fine, their glassware especially, and it was a straitened aristo indeed who did not possess antique table-settings rescued from some ruin or other. Sometimes one might find silver utensils in boxes, or useful tools, or coins. The coins were too plentiful to be worth much, individually, but they could be worked into buttons or other adornments. One of the high-born back at the Estate owned a saddle studded with copper pennies all from the year 2032. (I had occasionally been enlisted to polish it.)

But here also was the trash and inexplicable detritus: "plastic," gone brittle with sunlight or soft with the juices of the earth; bits of metal blooming with rust; electronic devices blackened by time and imbued with the sad inutility of a tensionless spring; engine parts, corroded; copper wire rotten with verdigris; aluminum cans and steel barrels eaten through by the poisonous fluids they had once contained—and so on, almost *ad infinitum*.

Here, too, were the in-between things, the curiosities, the ugly or pretty baubles, as intriguing and as useless as seashells. ("Put down that rusty trumpet, Adam, you'll cut your lip and poison your blood!"—my mother, when we had gone to the Tip many years before I met Julian. There had been no music in the trumpet anyway; its bell was bent and corroded through.)

More than that, though, there was the uneasy knowledge that these things, fine or corrupt, had survived their makers—had proved more imperishable than flesh or spirit (for the souls of the secular ancients were almost certainly not first in line for the Resurrection).

And yet, these books . . . they tempted; they proclaimed their seductions boldly. Some were decorated with impossibly beautiful women in various degrees of undress. I had already sacrificed my personal claim to virtue with certain young women at the Estate, whom I had recklessly kissed; at the age of seventeen I considered myself a jade, or something like one; but these images were so frank and impudent they made me blush and look away.

Julian simply ignored them, as he had always been invulnerable to the charms of women. He preferred the larger and more densely-written material—he had already set aside a textbook of BIOLOGY, spotted and discolored but largely intact. He found another volume almost as large, and handed it to me, saying, "Here, Adam, try this—you might find it enlightening."

I inspected it skeptically. The book was called A HISTORY OF MANKIND IN SPACE.

"The moon again," I said.

"Read it for yourself."

"Tissue of lies, I'm sure."

"With photographs."

"Photographs prove nothing. Those people could do anything with photographs."

"Well, read it anyway," Julian said.

In truth the idea excited me. We had had this argument many times, Julian and I, especially on autumn nights when the moon hung low and ponderous on the horizon. *People have walked there,* he would say. The first time he made this claim I laughed; the second time I said, "Yes, certainly: I once climbed there myself, on a greased rainbow—" But he had been serious.

Oh, I had heard these stories before. Who hadn't? Men on the moon. What surprised me was that someone as well-educated as Julian would believe them.

"Just take the book," he insisted.

"What: to keep?"

"Certainly to keep."

"Believe I will," I muttered, and I stuck the object in my back-satchel and felt both proud and guilty. What would my father say, if he knew I was reading literature without a Dominion stamp? What would my mother make of it? (Of course I would not tell them.)

At this point I backed off, and found a grassy patch a little away from the rubble, where I could sit and eat some of the lunch I had packed, and watch Julian, who continued to sort through the detritus with a kind of scholarly intensity. Sam Godwin came and joined me, brushing a spot on an old timber so he could recline without soiling his uniform, such as it was.

"He sure loves those old books," I said, making conversation.

Sam was often taciturn—the very picture of an old veteran—but he nodded and spoke familiarly: "He's learned to love them. I helped teach him. I wonder if that was wise. Maybe he loves them too much. It might be they'll kill him, one of these days."

"How, Sam? By the apostasy of them?"

"Julian's too smart for his own good. He debates with the Dominion clergy. Just last week I found him arguing with Ben Kreel* about God, history, and such abstractions. Which is precisely what he must *not* do, if he wants to survive the next few years."

"Why, what threatens him?"

"The jealousy of the powerful," Sam said, but he would say no more on the subject, only sat and stroked his graying beard, and glanced occasionally, and uneasily, to the east.

---

* Our local representative of the Council of the Dominion—in effect, the town's Mayor.

13

★　★　★

The day went on, and eventually Julian had to drag himself from his nest of books with only a pair of prizes: the INTRODUCTION TO BIOLOGY and another volume called GEOGRAPHY OF NORTH AMERICA. Time to go, Sam insisted; better to be back at the Estate by supper; in any case, riders had been sent ahead, and the official pickers and Dominion curators would soon be here to cull what we had left.

But I have said that Julian tutored me in one of his apostasies. Here is how it happened. We stopped, at the drowsy end of the afternoon, at the height of a ridge overlooking the town of Williams Ford, the grand Estate upstream of it, and the River Pine as it cut through the valley on its way from the mountains of the West. From this vantage we could see the steeple of the Dominion Hall, and the revolving wheels of the grist mill and the lumber mill, and so on, blue in the long light and hazy with woodsmoke, colored here and there with what remained of the autumn foliage. Far to the south a railway bridge crossed the gorge of the Pine like a suspended thread. *Go inside*, the weather seemed to proclaim; *it's fair but it won't be fair for long; bolt the window, stoke the fire, boil the apples; winter's due.* We rested our horses on the windy hilltop, and Julian found a blackberry bramble where the berries were still plump and dark, and we plucked some of these and ate them.

This was the world I had been born into. It was an autumn like every autumn I could remember. But I could not help thinking of the Tip and its ghosts. Maybe those people, the people

14

who had lived through the Efflorescence of Oil and the False Tribulation, had felt about their homes and neighborhoods as I felt about Williams Ford. They were ghosts to me, but they must have seemed real enough to themselves—must have *been* real; had not realized they were ghosts; and did that mean I was also a ghost, a revenant to haunt some future generation?

Julian saw my expression and asked me what was the matter. I told him my thoughts.

"Now you're thinking like a philosopher," he said, grinning.

"No wonder they're such a miserable brigade, then."

"Unfair, Adam—you've never seen a philosopher in your life." Julian believed in Philosophers and claimed to have met one or two.

"Well, I *imagine* they're miserable, if they go around thinking of themselves as ghosts and such."

"It's the condition of all things," Julian said. "This blackberry, for example." He plucked one and held it in the pale palm of his hand. "Has it always looked like this?"

"Obviously not," I said, impatiently.

"Once it was a tiny green bud of a thing, and before that it was part of the substance of the bramble, which before that was a seed inside a blackberry—"

"And round and round for all eternity."

"But no, Adam, that's the point. The bramble, and that tree over there, and the gourds in the field, and the crow circling over them—they're all descended from ancestors that didn't quite resemble them. A blackberry or a crow is a *form*, and forms change over time, the way clouds change shape as they travel across the sky."

15

"Forms of what?"

"Of DNA," Julian said earnestly. (The BIOLOGY he had picked out of the Tip was not the first BIOLOGY he had read.)

"Julian," Sam warned, "I once promised this boy's parents you wouldn't corrupt him."

I said, "I've heard of DNA. It's the life force of the secular ancients. And it's a myth."

"Like men walking on the moon?"

"Exactly."

"And who's your authority on this? Ben Kreel? The *Dominion History of the Union*?"

"Nothing is changeless except DNA? That's a peculiar argument even from you, Julian."

"It would be, if I were making it. But DNA *isn't* changeless. It struggles to remember itself, but it never remembers itself perfectly. Remembering a fish, it imagines a lizard. Remembering a horse, it imagines a hippopotamus. Remembering an ape, it imagines a man."

"Julian!" Sam was insistent now. "That's *quite* enough."

"You sound like a Darwinist," I said.

"Yes," Julian admitted, smiling in spite of his unorthodoxy, the autumn sun turning his face the color of penny copper. "I suppose I do."

That night, I lay in bed until I was reasonably certain both my parents were asleep. Then I rose, lit a lamp, and took the new (or rather, very old) HISTORY OF MANKIND IN SPACE from where I had hidden it behind my oaken dresser.

I leafed through the brittle pages. I didn't read the book. I *would* read it, but tonight I was too weary to pay close attention, and in any case I wanted to savor the words (lies and fictions though they might be), not rush through them. Tonight I wanted only to sample the book; in other words, to look at the pictures.

There were dozens of photographs, and each one captured my attention with fresh marvels and implausibilities. One of them showed—or purported to show—men standing on the surface of the moon, just as Julian had described.

The men in the picture were evidently Americans. They wore flags stitched to the shoulders of their moon clothing, an archaic version of our own flag, with something less than the customary sixty stars. Their clothing was white and ridiculously bulky, like the winter clothes of the Inuit, and they wore helmets with golden visors that disguised their faces. I supposed it must be very cold on the moon, if explorers required such cumbersome protection. They must have arrived in winter. However, there was no ice or snow in the neighborhood. The moon seemed to be little more than a desert, dry as a stick and dusty as a Tipman's wardrobe.

I cannot say how long I stared at this picture, puzzling over it. It might have been an hour or more. Nor can I accurately describe how it made me feel . . . larger than myself, but lonely, as if I had grown as tall as the stars and lost sight of everything familiar. By the time I closed the book the moon had risen outside my window—the *real* moon, I mean; a harvest moon, fat and orange, half-hidden behind drifting, evolving clouds.

I found myself wondering whether it was truly possible that men had visited that celestial body. Whether, as the pictures implied, they had ridden there on rockets, rockets a thousand times larger than the familiar Independence Day fireworks. But if men had visited the moon, why hadn't they stayed there? Was it so inhospitable a place that no one wished to remain?

Or perhaps they had stayed, and were living there still. If the moon was such a cold place, I reasoned, people residing on its surface would be forced to build fires to keep warm. There seemed to be no wood on the moon, judging by the photographs, so they must have resorted to coal or peat. I went to the window and examined the moon minutely for any sign of campfires, pit mining, or other lunar industry. But I could see none. It was only the moon, mottled and changeless. I blushed at my own gullibility, replaced the book in its hiding place, chased these heresies from my mind with a prayer (or a hasty facsimile of one), and eventually fell asleep.

3

IT FALLS TO ME TO EXPLAIN something of Williams Ford, and
my family's place in it—and Julian's—before I describe the threat
Sam Godwin feared, which materialized in our village not long
before Christmas.*

Situated at the head of the valley was the font of our prosperity,
the Duncan and Crowley Estate. It was a country estate (obviously, since we were in Athabaska, far from the eastern seats of
power), owned by two influential New York mercantile families,
who maintained their villa not only as a source of income but as a
kind of resort, safely distant (several days' journey by train) from
the intrigues and pestilences of city life. It was inhabited—ruled,
I might say—not only by the Duncan and Crowley patriarchs but
by a whole legion of cousins, nephews, relations by marriage, high-
born friends, and distinguished guests in search of clean air and
rural views. Our corner of Athabaska was blessed with a benign
climate and pleasant scenery, according to the season, and these
things attract idle aristos the way strong butter attracts flies.

---

* I beg the reader's patience if I detail matters that seem well-known. I
indulge the possibility of a foreign audience, or a posterity to whom our
present arrangements are not self-evident..

It remains unrecorded whether the town existed before the Estate or vice versa; but certainly the town depended on the Estate for its prosperity. In Williams Ford there were essentially three classes: the Owners, or aristos; below them the leasing class, who worked as smiths, carpenters, coopers, overseers, gardeners, beekeepers, etc., and whose leases were repaid in service; and finally the indentured laborers, who worked as field hands, inhabited rude shacks along the west bank of the Pine, and received no compensation beyond bad food and worse lodging.

My family occupied an ambivalent place in this hierarchy. My mother was a seamstress. She worked at the Estate as had her parents before her. My father, however, had arrived in Williams Ford as a transient, and his marriage to my mother had been controversial. He had "married a lease," as the saying has it, and had been taken on as a stable hand at the Estate in lieu of a dowry. The law allowed such unions, but popular opinion frowned on it. We had few friends of our own class, my mother's blood relations had since died (perhaps of embarrassment), and as a child I was often mocked and derided for my father's low origins.

On top of that was the issue of our religion. We were—because my father was—Church of Signs. In those days, every Christian church in America was required to have the formal approval of the Board of Registrars of the Dominion of Jesus Christ on Earth. (In popular parlance, "The Church of the Dominion," but this was a misnomer, since every church is a Dominion Church if it is recognized by the Board. Dominion Episcopal, Dominion Presbyterian, Dominion Baptist—even the Catholic Church of America since it renounced its fealty to the Roman Pope in

2112—all are included under the Dominionist umbrella, since the purpose of the Dominion is not to *be* a church but to *certify* churches. In America we are entitled by the Constitution to worship at any church we please, as long as it is a genuine Christian congregation and not some fraudulent or satanistic sect. The Board exists to make that distinction. Also to collect fees and tithes to further its important work.)

We were, as I said, Church of Signs, which was a marginal denomination, shunned by the leasing class, recognized but not fully endorsed by the Dominion, and popular mostly with illiterate indentured workers, among whom my father had been raised. Our faith took for its master text that passage in Mark which proclaims, "In my Name they will cast out devils, and speak in new tongues; they will handle serpents, and if they drink poison they will not be sickened by it." We were snake-handlers, in other words, and famous beyond our modest numbers for it. Our congregation consisted of a dozen farmhands, mostly transients lately arrived from the southern states. My father was its deacon (though we did not use that name), and we kept snakes, for ritual purposes, in wire cages on our back acre, next to the outbuilding. This practice contributed very little to our social standing.

That had been the situation of our family when Julian Comstock arrived as a guest of the Duncan and Crowley families, along with his mentor Sam Godwin, and when Julian and I met by coincidence while hunting.

At that time I had been apprenticed to my father, who had risen to the rank of an overseer at the Estate's lavish and extensive stables. My father loved animals, especially horses. Unfortunately I was not made in the same mold, and my relations with the stable's equine inhabitants rarely extended beyond a brisk mutual tolerance. I did not love my job—which consisted largely of sweeping straw, shoveling ordure, and doing in general those chores the older stablehands felt to be beneath their dignity—so I was pleased when it became customary for a household amanuensis (or even Sam Godwin in person) to arrive and summon me away from my work at Julian's request. (Since the request emanated from a Comstock it couldn't be overruled, no matter how fiercely the grooms and saddlers gnashed their teeth to see me escape their autocracy.)

At first we met to read and discuss books, or hunt together; later, Sam Godwin invited me to audit Julian's lessons, for he had been charged with Julian's education as well as his general welfare. (I had been taught the rudiments of reading and writing at the Dominion school, and refined these skills under the tutelage of my mother, who believed in the power of literacy as an improving force. My father could neither read nor write.) And it was not more than a year after our first acquaintance that Sam presented himself one evening at my parents' cottage with an extraordinary proposal.

"Mr. and Mrs. Hazzard," Sam had said, putting his hand up to touch his cap (which he had removed when he entered the cottage, so that the gesture looked like a salute), "you know of course about the friendship between your son and Julian Comstock."

"Yes," my mother said. "And worry over it often enough—matters at the Estate being what they are."

My mother was a small woman, plump, but forceful, with ideas of her own. My father, who spoke seldom, on this occasion spoke not at all, only sat in his chair holding a laurel-root pipe, which he did not light.

"Matters at the Estate are exactly the crux of the issue," Sam Godwin said. "I'm not sure how much Adam has told you about our situation there. Julian's father, General Bryce Comstock, who was my friend as well as my commanding officer, shortly before his death charged me with Julian's care and well-being—"

"Before his death," my mother pointed out, "at the gallows, for treason."

Sam winced. "True, Mrs. Hazzard, I can't deny it, but I assert my belief that the trial was rigged and the verdict indefensible. Defensible or not, however, it doesn't alter my obligation as far as the son is concerned. I promised to care for the boy, Mrs. Hazzard, and I mean to keep my promise."

"A Christian sentiment." Her skepticism was not entirely disguised.

"As for your implication about the Estate, and the practices of the young heirs and heiresses there, I couldn't agree more. Which is why I approved and encouraged Julian's friendship with your son. Apart from Adam, Julian has no true friends. The Estate is such a den of venomous snakes—no offense," he added, remembering our religious affiliation, and making the common but mistaken assumption that congregants of the Church of Signs necessarily *like* snakes, or feel some kinship with them—"no offense, but I would sooner allow Julian to associate with, uh, scorpions," striking for a more palatable simile, "than abandon him to the sneers, machinations, ruses, and ruinous habits of his peers. That makes me not only his teacher but his constant companion. But I'm almost three times his age, Mrs. Hazzard, and he needs a reliable friend more nearly of his own growth."

"What do you propose, exactly, Mr. Godwin?"

"What I propose is that I take on Adam as a second student, full-time, and to the ultimate benefit of both boys."

Sam was usually a man of few words—even as a teacher—and he seemed as exhausted by this oration as if he had lifted some great weight.

"As a student, but a student of *what*, Mr. Godwin?"

"Mechanics. History. Grammar and composition. Martial skills—"

"Adam already knows how to fire a rifle."

"Pistolwork, sabrework, fist-fighting—but that's only a fraction of it," Sam added hastily. "Julian's father asked me to cultivate the boy's mind as well as his reflexes."

My mother had more to say on the subject, chiefly about how my work at the stables helped offset the family's leases, and how difficult it would be to do without those extra vouchers at the Estate store. But Sam had anticipated the point. He had been entrusted by Julian's mother—that is to say, the sister-in-law of the President—with a discretionary fund for Julian's education, which could be tapped to compensate for my absence from the stables. And at a handsome rate. He quoted a number, and the objections from my parents grew considerably less strenuous, and were finally whittled away to nothing. (I observed all this from a room away, through a gap in the door.)

Which is not to say no misgivings remained. Before I set off for the Estate the next day, this time to visit one of the Great Houses rather than the stables, my mother warned me not to tangle myself too tightly with the affairs of the high-born. I promised her I would cling to my Christian virtues. (A hasty promise, less easily kept than I imagined.*)

"It may not be your morals that are at risk," she said. "The high-born conduct themselves by different standards than we use, Adam. The games they play have mortal stakes. You do know that Julian's father was hung?"

Julian never spoke of it, but it was a matter of public record. I repeated Sam's assertion that Bryce Comstock had been innocent.

"He may well have been. That's the point. There has been a Comstock in the Presidency for the past thirty years, and the current Comstock is said to be jealous of his power. The only real threat to the reign of Julian's uncle was the ascendancy of his brother, who made himself dangerously popular in the war

---

* Julian's somewhat feminine nature had won him a reputation among the other young aristos as a sodomite. That they could believe this of him without evidence is testimony to the tenor of their thoughts, as a class. But it had occasionally rebounded to my benefit. On more than one occasion, his female acquaintances—sophisticated girls of my own age, or older—made the assumption that I was Julian's intimate companion, in a *physical* sense. Whereupon they undertook to cure me of my deviant habits, in the most direct fashion. I was happy to cooperate with these "cures," and they were successful, every time.

with the Brazilians. I suspect Mr. Godwin is correct, that Bryce Comstock was hanged not because he was a *bad* General but because he was a *successful* one."

No doubt such scandals were possible—I had heard stories about life in New York City, where the President resided, that would curl a Cynic's hair. But what could these things possibly have to do with me? Or even Julian? We were only boys.

Such was my naiveté.

4

THE DAYS HAD GROWN SHORT, and Thanksgiving had come
and gone, and so had November, and snow was in the air—the
tang of it, anyway—when fifty cavalrymen of the Athabaska
Reserve rode into Williams Ford, escorting an equal number of
Campaigners and Poll-Takers.

Many people despised the Athabaskan winter. I was not
one of them. I didn't mind the cold and the darkness, not so
long as there was a hard-coal heater, a spirit lamp to read by
on long nights, and the chance of wheat cakes or headcheese
for breakfast. And Christmas was coming up fast—one of the
four Universal Christian Holidays recognized by the Dominion
(the others being Easter, Independence Day, and Thanksgiving).
My favorite of these had always been Christmas. It was not so
much the gifts, which were generally meager—though last year
I had received from my parents the lease of a muzzle-loading
rifle of which I was exceptionally proud—nor was it entirely the
spiritual substance of the holiday, which I am ashamed to say
seldom entered my mind except when it was thrust upon me at
religious services. What I loved was the combined effect of brisk
air, frost-whitened mornings, pine and holly wreaths pinned to
doorways, cranberry-red banners draped above the main street

to flap cheerfully in the cold wind, carols and hymns chanted or sung—the whole breathless confrontation with Winter, half defiance and half submission. I liked the clockwork regularity of these rituals, as if a particular cog on the wheel of time had engaged with neat precision. It soothed; it spoke of eternity.

But this was an ill-omened season.

The Reserve troops rode into town on the fifteenth of December. Ostensibly, they were here to conduct the Presidential Election. National elections were a formality in Williams Ford. By the time our citizens were polled, the outcome was usually a foregone conclusion, already decided in the populous Eastern states—that is, when there was more than one candidate, which was seldom. For the last six electoral years no individual or party had contested the election, and we had been ruled by one Comstock or another for three decades. *Election* had become indistinguishable from *acclamation*.

But that was all right, because an election was still a momentous event, almost a kind of circus, involving the arrival of Poll-Takers and Campaigners, who always had a fine show to put on.

And this year—the rumor emanated from high chambers of the Estate, and had been whispered everywhere—there was to be a movie shown in the Dominion Hall.

I had never seen any movies, though Julian had described them to me. He had seen them often in New York when he was younger, and whenever he grew nostalgic—life in Williams Ford was sometimes a little sedate for Julian's taste—it was the movies he was provoked to mention. And so, when the showing of a movie was announced as part of the electoral process, both of us were excited, and we agreed to meet behind the Dominion Hall at the appointed hour.

Neither of us had any legitimate reason to be there. I was too young to vote, and Julian would have been conspicuous and perhaps unwelcome as the only aristo at a gathering of the leasing class. (The high-born had been polled independently at the Estate, and had already voted proxies for their indentured labor.) So I let my parents leave for the Hall early in the evening, and I followed surreptitiously, on foot, and arrived just before the event was scheduled to begin. I waited behind the meeting hall, where a dozen horses were tethered, until Julian arrived on an animal borrowed from the Estate stables. He was dressed in his best approximation of a leaser's clothing: hempen shirt and trousers of a dark color, and a black felt hat with its brim pulled low to disguise his face.

He dismounted, looking troubled, and I asked him what was wrong. Julian shook his head. "Nothing, Adam—or nothing *yet*— but Sam says there's trouble brewing." And here he regarded me with an expression verging on pity. "War," he said.

"There's always war."

"A new offensive."

"Well, what of it? Labrador's a million miles away."

"Obviously your sense of geography hasn't been much improved by Sam's classes. And we might be *physically* a long distance from the front, but we're *operationally* far too close for comfort."

I didn't know what that meant, and so I dismissed it. "We can worry about that after the movie, Julian."

He forced a grin and said, "Yes, I suppose so. As well after as before."

So we entered the Dominion Hall just as the lamps were being dimmed, and slouched into the last row of crowded pews, and waited for the show to start.

There was a broad stage at the front of the Hall, from which all religious appurtenances had been removed, and a square white screen had been erected in place of the usual pulpit or dais. On each side of the screen was a kind of tent in which the two players sat, with their scripts and dramatic gear: speaking-horns, bells, blocks, a drum, a pennywhistle, *et alia*. This was, Julian said, a stripped-down edition of what one might find in a fashionable New York movie theater. In the city, the screen (and thus the images projected on it) would be larger; the players would be more professional, since script-reading and noise-making were considered fashionable arts, and the city players competed with one another for roles; and there might be a third player stationed behind the screen for dramatic narration or additional "sound effects." There might even be an orchestra, with thematic music written for each individual production.

Movies were devised in such a way that two main characters, male and female, could be voiced by the players, with the male actor photographed so that he appeared on the left during dialogue scenes, and the female actor on the right. The players would observe the movie by a system of mirrors, and could follow scripts illuminated by a kind of binnacle lamp (so as not to cast a distracting light), and they spoke their lines as the photographed actors spoke, so that their voices seemed to emanate from the screen. Likewise, their drumming and bell-ringing and such corresponded to events within the movie.*

"Of course, they did it better in the secular era," Julian whispered, and I prayed no one had overheard this indelicate comment. By all reports, movies had indeed been spectacular during the Efflorescence of Oil—with recorded sound, natural color rather than black-and-gray, etc. But they were also (by the same reports) hideously impious, blasphemous to the extreme, and routinely pornographic. Fortunately (or *unfortunately*, from Julian's point of view) no examples have survived; the media on which they were recorded was ephemeral; the film stock has long since rotted, and "digital" copies are degraded and wholly undecodable. These movies belonged to the twentieth and early twenty-first centuries—that period of great, unsustainable, and hedonistic prosperity, driven by the burning of Earth's reserves of perishable oil, which culminated in the False Tribulation, and the wars, and the plagues, and the painful dwindling of inflated populations to more reasonable numbers.

Our truest and best American antiquity, as the *Dominion History of the Union* insisted, was the nineteenth century, whose

---

* The illusion was quite striking when the players were professional, but their lapses could be equally astonishing. Julian once recounted to me a New York movie production of Wm. Shakespeare's *Hamlet*, in which a player had come to the theater inebriated, causing the unhappy Denmark to seem to exclaim "Sea of troubles—(an unprintable oath)—I have troubles of my own," with more obscenities, and much inappropriate bell-ringing and vulgar whistling, until an understudy could be hurried out to replace him.

household virtues and modest industries we have been forced by circumstance imperfectly to restore, whose skills were practical, and whose literature was often useful and improving.

But I have to confess that some of Julian's apostasy had infected me. I was troubled by unhappy thoughts even as the torchieres were extinguished and Ben Kreel (our Dominion representative, in effect the town's mayor, standing in front of the movie screen) delivered a brief lecture on Nation, Piety, and Duty. *War*, Julian had said, implying not just the everlasting War in Labrador but a new phase of it, one that might reach its skeletal hand right into Williams Ford—and then what of me, and what of my family?

"We are here to cast our ballots," Ben Kreel said in summation, "a sacred duty at once to our country and our faith, a country so successfully and benevolently stewarded by its leader, President Deklan Comstock, whose Campaigners, I see by the motions of their hands, are anxious to get on with the events of the night; and so, without further adieu, etc., please direct your attention to the presentation of their moving picture, *First Under Heaven*, which they have prepared for our enjoyment—"

The necessary gear had been hauled into Williams Ford under a canvas-top wagon: a projection apparatus and a portable Swiss dynamo (probably captured from the Dutch forces in Labrador), powered by distilled spirits, installed in a sort of trench or redoubt freshly dug behind the church to muffle its sound, which nevertheless penetrated through the plank floors like the growl of a huge dog. This vibration only added to the sense of moment, as the last illuminating flame was extinguished and the electric bulb within the huge black mechanical projector flared up.

The movie began. As it was the first I had ever seen, my astonishment was complete. I was so entranced by the illusion of photographs "come to life" that the substance of the scenes almost
escaped me . . . but I remember an ornate title, and scenes of the
Second Battle of Quebec, recreated by actors but utterly real to
me, accompanied by drum-banging and shrill pennywhistling to
represent the reports of shot and shell. Those at the front of the
auditorium flinched instinctively; several of the village's promi-
nent women came near to fainting, and clasped the hands or
arms of their male companions, who might be as bruised, come
morning, as if they had participated in the battle itself.

Soon enough, however, the Dutchmen under their cross-and-
laurel flag began to retreat from the American forces, and an
actor representing the young Deklan Comstock came to the
fore, reciting his Vows of Inauguration (a bit prematurely, but
history was here truncated for the purposes of art)—that's the
one in which he mentions both the Continental Imperative and
the Debt to the Past. He was voiced, of course, by one of the
players, a *basso profundo* whose tones emerged from his speaking-
bell with ponderous gravity. (Which was also a slight revision of
the truth, for the genuine Deklan Comstock possessed a high-
pitched voice, and was prone to petulance.)

The movie then proceeded to more decorous episodes and
scenic views representing the glories of the reign of Deklan
Conqueror, as he was known to the Army of the Laurentians,
which had marched him to his ascendancy in New York City.
Here was the reconstruction of Washington, DC (a project
never completed, always in progress, hindered by a swampy

climate and insect-borne diseases); here was the Illumination of Manhattan, whereby electric streetlights were powered by a hydroelectric dynamo, four hours every day between 6 and 10 p.m.; here was the military shipyard at Boston Harbor, the coal mines and foundries and weapons factories of Pennsylvania, the newest and shiniest steam engines to pull the newest and shiniest trains, etc., etc.

I had to wonder at Julian's reaction to all this. This entire show, after all, was concocted to extol the virtues of the man who had contrived the death by hanging of his father. I could not forget—and Julian must be constantly aware—that the current President was a fratricidal tyrant. But Julian's eyes were riveted on the screen. This reflected (I later learned) not his opinion of contemporary politics but his fascination with what he preferred to call "cinema." This making of illusions in two dimensions was never far from his mind—it was, perhaps, his "true calling," and would culminate in the creation of Julian's suppressed cinematic masterwork, *The Life and Adventures of the Great Naturalist Charles Darwin* . . . but that tale remains for another telling.

The present movie went on to mention the successful forays against the Brazilians at Panama during Deklan Conqueror's reign, which may have struck closer to home, for I saw Julian wince once or twice.

As for me . . . I tried to lose myself in the moment, but my attention was woefully truant.

Perhaps it was the strangeness of the campaign event, so close to Christmas. Perhaps it was the HISTORY OF MANKIND IN SPACE, which I had been reading in bed, a page or two at a time, almost every night since our journey to the Tip. Whatever the cause, I was beset by a sudden anxiety and sense of melancholy. Here I was in the midst of everything that seemed familiar and ought to be comforting—the crowd of the leasing class, the enclosing benevolence of the Dominion Hall, the banners and tokens of the Christmas season—and it all felt suddenly *ephemeral*, as if the world were a bucket from which the bottom had dropped out.

Perhaps this was what Julian had called "the philosopher's perspective." If so, I wondered how the philosophers endured it. I had learned a little from Sam Godwin—and more from Julian, who read books of which even Sam disapproved—about the discredited ideas of the Secular Era. I thought of Einstein, and his insistence that no particular point of view was more privileged than any other: in other words his "general relativity," and its claim that the answer to the question "What is real?" begins with the question "Where are you standing?" Was that all I was, here in the cocoon of Williams Ford—a Point of View? Or was I an incarnation of a molecule of DNA, "imperfectly remembering," as Julian had said, an ape, a fish, and an amoeba? Maybe even the Nation that Ben Kreel had praised so extravagantly was only an example of this trend in nature—an imperfect memory of another century, which had itself been an imperfect memory of all the centuries before it, and so back to the dawn of Man (in Eden, or Africa, as Julian believed).

Perhaps this was just my growing disenchantment with the town where I had been raised—or a presentiment that it was about to be stolen away from me.

★ ★ ★

The movie ended with a stirring scene of an American flag, its thirteen stripes and sixty stars rippling in sunlight—betokening, the narrator insisted, another four years of the prosperity and benevolence engendered by the rule of Deklan Conqueror, for whom the audience's votes were solicited, not that there was any competing candidate known or rumored. The film flapped against its reel; the electric bulb was extinguished. Then the deacons of the Dominion began to reignite the wall lights. Several of the men in the audience had lit pipes during the cinematic display, and their smoke mingled with the smudge of the torchieres, a blue-gray thundercloud hovering under the high arches of the ceiling.

Julian seemed distracted, and slumped in his pew with his hat pulled low. "Adam," he whispered, "we have to find a way out of here."

"I believe I see one," I said; "it's called the door—but what's the hurry?"

"Look at the door more closely. Two men of the Reserve have been posted there."

I looked, and what he had said was true. "But isn't that just to protect the balloting?" For Ben Kreel had retaken the stage and was preparing to ask for a formal show of hands.

"Tom Shearney, the barber with a bladder complaint, just tried to leave to use the jakes. He was turned back."

Indeed, Tom Shearney was seated less than a yard away from us, squirming unhappily and casting resentful glances at the Reserve men.

"But after the balloting—"

"This isn't about balloting. This is about conscription."

"Conscription!"

"Hush!" Julian said hastily, shaking his hair out of his pale face. "You'll start a stampede. I didn't think it would begin so soon . . . but we've had certain telegrams from New York about setbacks in Labrador, and the call-up of new divisions. Once the balloting is finished the Campaigners will probably announce a recruitment drive, and take the names of everyone present and survey them for the names and ages of their children."

"We're too young to be drafted," I said, for we were both just seventeen.

"Not according to what I've heard. The rules have been changed. Oh, you can probably find a way to hide out when the culling begins—and get away with it, considering how far we are from anywhere else. But *my* presence here is well-known. I don't have a mob or family to melt away into. In fact it's probably not a coincidence that so many Reserves have been sent to such a little village as Williams Ford."

"What do you mean, not a coincidence?"

"My uncle has never been happy about my existence. He has no children of his own. No heirs. He sees me as a possible competitor for the Executive."

"But that's absurd. You don't *want* to be President—do you?"

"I would sooner shoot myself. But Uncle Deklan has a jealous bent, and he distrusts the motives of my mother in protecting me."

"How does a draft help him?"

"The entire draft is not aimed at me, but I'm sure he finds it a useful tool. If I'm drafted, no one can complain that he's excepting his own family from the general conscription. And when he has me in the infantry he can be sure I find myself on the front lines in Labrador—performing some noble but suicidal trench attack."

"But—Julian! Can't Sam protect you?"

"Sam is a retired soldier; he has no power except what arises from the patronage of my mother. Which isn't worth much in the coin of the present realm. Adam, is there another way out of this building?"

"Only the door, unless you mean to break a pane of that colored glass that fills the windows."

"Somewhere to hide, then?"

I thought about it. "Maybe," I said. "There's a room behind the stage where the religious equipment is stored. You can enter it from the wings. We could hide there, but it has no door of its own."

"It'll have to do. If we can get there without attracting attention."

But that was not too difficult, for the torchieres had not all been re-lit, much of the hall was still in shadow, and the audience was milling about a bit, and stretching, while the Campaigners prepared to record the vote that was to follow—they were meticulous accountants even though the final tally was a foregone conclusion and the ballrooms were already booked for Deklan Conqueror's latest inauguration. Julian and I shuffled from one shadow to another, giving no appearance of haste, until we were close to the foot of the stage; there we paused at an entrance to the storage room, until a goonish Reserve man who had been eyeing us was called away by a superior officer to help dismantle the projecting equipment. We ducked through the curtained door into near-absolute darkness. Julian stumbled over some obstruction (a piece of the church's tack piano, which had been disassembled for cleaning in 2165 by a traveling piano-mechanic, who had died of a stroke before finishing the job), the result being a woody "clang!" that seemed loud enough to alert the whole occupancy of the church, but evidently didn't.

What little light there was came through a high glazed window that was hinged so that it could be opened in summer for purposes of ventilation. It was a weak sort of illumination, for the night was cloudy, and only the torches along the main street were shining. But it registered as our eyes adjusted to the dimness. "Perhaps we can get out that way," Julian said.

"Not without a ladder. Although—"

"What? Speak up, Adam, if you have an idea."

"This is where they store the risers—the long wooden blocks the choir stands on when they're racked up for a performance. Perhaps those—"

But he was already examining the shadowy contents of the storage room, as intently as he had surveyed the Tip for ancient books. We found the likely suspects, and managed to stack them to a useful height without causing too much noise. (In the church hall, the Campaigners had already registered a unanimous vote for Deklan Comstock and had begun to break the news about the conscription drive. Some few voices were raised in futile objection; Ben Kreel was calling loudly for calm—no one heard us rearranging the unused furniture.)

The window was at least ten feet high, and almost too narrow to crawl through, and when we emerged on the other side we had to hang by our fingertips before dropping to the ground. I bent my right ankle awkwardly as I landed, though no lasting harm was done.

The night, already cold, had turned colder. We were near the hitching posts, and the horses whinnied at our surprising arrival and blew steam from their gaping nostrils. A fine, gritty snow had begun to fall. There was not much wind, however, and Christmas banners hung limply in the frigid air.

Julian made straight for his horse and loosed its reins from the post. "What are we going to do?" I asked.

"You, Adam, will do nothing but protect your own existence as best you know how; while I—"

But he balked at pronouncing his plans, and a shadow of anxiety passed over his face. Events were moving rapidly in the realm of the aristos, events I could barely comprehend.

"We can wait them out," I said, a little desperately. "The Reserves can't stay in Williams Ford forever."

"No. Unfortunately neither can I, for Deklan Conqueror knows where to find me, and has made up his mind to remove me from the game of politics like a captured chesspiece."

"But where will you go? And what—"

He put a finger to his mouth. There was a noise from the front of the Dominion Church Hall, as of the doors being thrown open, and voices of congregants arguing or wailing over the news of the conscription drive. "Ride with me," Julian said. "Quick, now!"

We did not follow the main street, but caught a path that turned behind the blacksmith's barn and through the wooded border of the River Pine, north in the general direction of the Estate. The night was dark, and the horses stepped slowly, but they knew the path almost by instinct, and some light from the town still filtered through the thinly falling snow, which touched my face like a hundred small cold fingers.

"It was never possible that I could stay at Williams Ford forever," Julian said. "You ought to have known that, Adam."

Truly, I should have. It was Julian's constant theme, after all: the impermanence of things. I had always put this down to the circumstances of his childhood, the death of his father, the separation from his mother, the kind but aloof tutelage of Sam Godwin.

But I could not help thinking once more of the HISTORY OF MANKIND IN SPACE and the photographs in it—not of the First Men on the Moon, who were Americans, but of the Last Visitors to that celestial sphere, who had been Chinamen, and whose "space suits" had been firecracker-red. Like the Americans, they had planted their flag in expectation of more visitations to come; but the End of Oil and the False Tribulation had put paid to those plans.

And I thought of the even lonelier Plains of Mars, photographed by machines (or so the book alleged) but never touched by human feet. The universe, it seemed, was full to brimming with lonesome places. Somehow I had stumbled into one. The snow squall ended; the uninhabited moon came through the clouds; and the winter fields of Williams Ford glowed with an unearthly luminescence.

"If you must leave," I said, "let me come with you."

"No," Julian said promptly. He had pulled his hat down around his ears, to protect himself from the cold, and I couldn't see much of his face, but his eyes shone when he glanced in my direction. "Thank you, Adam. I wish it were possible. But it isn't. You must stay here, and dodge the draft, if possible, and polish your literary skills, and one day write books, like Mr. Charles Curtis Easton."

That was my ambition, which had grown over the last year, nourished by our mutual love of books and by Sam Godwin's exercises in English Composition, for which I had discovered an unexpected talent.* At the moment it seemed a petty dream. Evanescent. Like all dreams. Like life itself. "None of that matters," I said.

---

* Not a talent that was born fully-formed, I should add. Only two years previously I had presented to Sam Godwin my first finished story, which I had called "A Western Boy: His Adventures in Enemy Europe." Sam had praised its style and ambition, but called attention to a number of flaws: elephants, for instance, were not native to Brussels, and were generally too massive to be wrestled to the ground by American lads; a journey from London to Rome could not be accomplished in a matter of hours, even on "a very fast horse"—and Sam might have continued in this vein, had I not fled the room in a condition of acute auctorial embarrassment.

"That's where you're wrong," Julian said. "You must not make the mistake of thinking that because nothing lasts, nothing matters."

"Isn't that the philosopher's point of view?"

"Not if the philosopher knows what he's talking about." Julian reined up his horse and turned to face me, something of the imperiousness of his famous family entering into his mien. "Listen, Adam, there is something important you can do for me—at some personal risk. Are you willing?"

"Yes," I said immediately.

"Then listen closely. Before long the Reserves will be watching the roads out of Williams Ford, if they aren't already. I have to leave, and I have to leave tonight. I won't be missed until morning, and then, at least at first, only by Sam. What I want you to do is this: go home—your parents will be worried about the conscription, and you can try to calm them down—but don't allude to any of what happened tonight—and first thing in the morning, make your way as inconspicuously as possible into the Estate and find Sam. Tell him what happened at the Church Hall, and tell him to ride out of town as soon as he can do so without being caught. Tell him he can find me at Lundsford. That's the message."

"Lundsford? There's nothing at Lundsford."

"Precisely: nothing important enough that the Reserves would think to look for us there. You remember what the Tipman said in the fall, about the place he found those books? A low place near the main excavations. Sam can look for me there."

"I'll tell him," I promised, blinking against the cold wind, which irritated my eyes.

"Thank you, Adam," he said gravely. "For everything." Then he forced a smile, and for a moment was just Julian, the friend with whom I had hunted squirrels and spun tales: "Merry Christmas," he said. "Happy New Year!"

And wheeled his horse about, and rode away.

5

THERE IS A DOMINION CEMETERY in Williams Ford, and I passed it on the ride back home—carved stones sepulchral in the moonlight—but my sister Flaxie was not buried there.

As I have said, the Church of Signs was tolerated but not endorsed by the Dominion. We were not entitled to plots in the Dominion yard. Flaxie had a place in the acreage behind our cottage, marked by a modest wooden cross, but the cemetery put me in mind of Flaxie nonetheless, and after I returned the horse to the barn I stopped by Flaxie's grave (despite the shivery cold) and tipped my hat to her, the way I had always tipped my hat to her in life.

Flaxie had been a bright, impudent, mischievous small thing— as golden-haired as her nickname implied. (Her given name was Dolores, but she was always Flaxie to me.) The Pox had taken her quite suddenly and, as these things go, mercifully. I didn't remember her death; I had been down with the same Pox, though I had survived it. What I remembered was waking up from my fever into a house gone strangely quiet. No one had wanted to tell me about Flaxie, but I had seen my mother's tormented eyes, and I knew the truth without having to be told. Death had played lottery with us, and Flaxie had drawn the short straw.

(It is, I think, for the likes of Flaxie that we maintain a belief in Heaven. I have met very few adults, outside the enthusiasts of the established Church, who genuinely believe in Heaven, and Heaven was scant consolation for my grieving mother. But Flaxie, who was five, had believed in it fervently—imagined it was something like a meadow, with wildflowers blooming, and a perpetual summer picnic underway—and if that childish belief soothed her in her extremity, then it served a purpose more noble than truth.)

Tonight the cottage was almost as quiet as it had been during the mourning that followed Flaxie's death. I came through the door to find my mother dabbing her eyes with a handkerchief, and my father frowning over his pipe, which, uncharacteristically, he had filled and lit. "The draft," he said.

"Yes," I said. "I heard about it."

My mother was too distraught to speak. My father said, "We'll do what we can to protect you, Adam. But—"

"I'm not afraid to serve my country," I said.

"That's a praiseworthy attitude," my father said glumly, and my mother wept even harder. "But we don't yet know what might be necessary. Maybe the situation in Labrador isn't as bad as it seems."

Scant of words though my father was, I had often enough relied on him for advice, which he had freely given. He was fully aware, for instance, of my distaste for snakes—for which reason, abetted by my mother, I had been allowed to avoid the sacraments of our faith, and the venomous swellings and occasional amputations inflicted upon other parishioners—and, while this

46

disappointed him, he had nevertheless taught me the practical aspects of snake-handling, including how to grasp a serpent in such a way as to avoid its bite, and how to kill one, should the necessity arise.* He was a practical man despite his unusual beliefs.

But he had no advice to offer me tonight. He looked like a hunted man who has come to the end of a cul-de-sac, and can neither go forward nor turn back.

I went to my bedroom, although I doubted I would be able to sleep. Instead—without any real plan in mind—I bundled a few of my possessions for easy carrying. My squirrel-gun, chiefly, and some notes and writing, and A HISTORY OF MANKIND IN SPACE; and I thought I should add some salted pork, or something of that nature, but I resolved to wait until later, so my mother wouldn't see me packing.

Before dawn, I put on several layers of clothing and a heavy pak-ool hat, rolled down so the wool covered my ears. I opened the window of my room and clambered over the sill and closed the glass behind me, after I had retrieved my rifle and gear. Then I crept across the open yard to the barn, and saddled up a horse

---

* "Grasp it where its neck ought to be, behind the head; ignore the tail, however it may thrash; and crack its skull, hard and often enough to subdue it." I had recounted these instructions to Julian, whose horror of serpents far exceeded my own: "Oh, I could never do such a thing!" he had exclaimed. This surfeit of timidity may surprise readers who have followed his later career.

(the gelding named Rapture, who was the fastest, though this would leave my father's rig an animal shy), and rode out under a sky that had just begun to show first light.

Last night's brief snowfall still covered the ground. I was not the first up this winter morning, and the cold air already smelled of Christmas. The bakery in Williams Ford was busy making nativity cakes and cinnamon buns. The sweet, yeasty smell filled the northwest end of town like an intoxicating fog, for there was no wind to carry it away. The day was dawning blue and still.

Signs of Christmas were everywhere—as they ought to be, for today was the Eve of that universal holiday—but so was evidence of the conscription drive. The Reservists were already awake, passing like shadows in their scruffy uniforms, and a crowd of them had gathered by the hardware store. They had hung out a faded flag and posted a sign, which I could not read, because I was determined to keep a distance between myself and the soldiers; but I knew a recruiting-post when I saw one. I did not doubt that the main ways in and out of town had been put under close observation.

I took a back way to the Estate, the same riverside road Julian and I had traveled the night before. Because of the lack of wind, our tracks were undisturbed. We were the only ones who had recently passed this way. Rapture was revisiting his own hoof-prints.

Close to the Estate, but still within a concealing grove of pines, I lashed the horse to a sapling and proceeded on foot.

The Duncan-Crowley Estate was not fenced, for there was no real demarcation of its boundaries; under the Leasing System, everything in Williams Ford was owned (in the legal sense) by the two great families. I approached from the western side, which was half-wooded and used by the aristos for casual riding and hunting. This morning the copse was not inhabited, and I saw no one until I had passed the snow-mounded hedges which marked the beginning of the formal gardens. Here, in summer, apple and cherry trees blossomed and produced fruit; flowerbeds gave forth symphonies of color and scent; bees nursed in languid ecstasies. But now it was barren, the paths quilted with snow, and there was no one visible but the senior groundskeeper, sweeping the wooden portico of the nearest of the Estate's several Great Houses.

The Houses were dressed for Christmas. Christmas was a grander event at the Estate than in the town proper, as might be expected. The winter population of the Duncan-Crowley Estate was not as large as its summer population, but there was still a number of both families, plus whatever cousins and hangers-on had elected to hibernate over the cold season. Sam Godwin, as Julian's tutor, was not permitted to sleep in either of the two most luxurious buildings, but bunked among the elite staff in a white-pillared house that would have passed for a mansion anywhere but here. This was where he had conducted classes for Julian and me, and I knew the building intimately. It, too, was dressed for Christmas; a holly wreath hung on the door; pine boughs were suspended over the lintels; a Banner of the Cross dangled from the eaves. The door was not locked, and I let myself in quietly.

It was still early in the morning, at least as the aristos and their elite helpers calculated time. The tiled entranceway was empty and still. I went straight for the rooms where Sam Godwin slept and conducted his classes, down an oaken corridor lit only by the dawn filtering through a window at the long end. The floor was carpeted and gave no sound, though my shoes left damp footprints behind me.

At Sam's particular door, I was confronted with a dilemma. I could not knock, for fear of alerting others. My mission as I saw it was to deliver Julian's message as discreetly as possible. But neither could I walk in on a sleeping man—could I?

I tried the handle of the door. It moved freely. I opened the door a fraction of an inch, meaning to whisper, "Sam?"—and give him some warning.

But I could hear Sam's voice, low and muttering, as if he were talking to himself. I listened more closely. The words seemed strange. He was speaking in a guttural language, not English. Perhaps he wasn't alone. It was too late to back away, however, so I decided to brazen it out. I opened the door entirely and stepped inside, saying, "Sam! It's me, Adam. I have a message from Julian—"

I stopped short, alarmed by what I saw. Sam Godwin—the same gruff but familiar Sam who had taught me the rudiments of history and geography—was practicing *black magic,* or some other form of witchcraft: *on Christmas Eve!* He wore a striped cowl about his shoulders, and leather lacings on his arm, and a boxlike implement strapped to his forehead; and his hands were upraised over an arrangement of nine candles mounted in a brass holder that appeared to have been scavenged from some ancient Tip. The invocation he had been murmuring seemed to echo through the room: Bah-*rook*-a-*tah*-atten-*eye*-hello-*hey*-noo . . .

My jaw dropped.

"Adam!" Sam said, almost as startled as I was, and he quickly pulled the shawl from his back and began to unlace his various unholy riggings.

This was so irregular I could barely comprehend it.

Then I was afraid I *did* comprehend it. Often enough in Dominion school I had heard Ben Kreel speak about the vices and wickedness of the Secular Era, some of which still lingered, he said, in the cities of the East—irreverence, irreligiosity, skepticism, occultism, depravity. And I thought of the ideas I had so casually imbibed from Julian and (indirectly) from Sam, some of which I had even begun to believe: Einsteinism, Darwinism, space travel . . . had I been seduced by the outrunners of some New Yorkish paganism? Had I been duped by Philosophy?

"A message," Sam said, concealing his heathenish gear, "what message? Where is Julian?"

But I could not stay. I fled the room.

Sam barreled out of the house after me. I was fast, but he was long-legged and conditioned by his military career, strong for all his forty-odd years, and he caught me in the winter gardens—tackled me from behind. I kicked and tried to pull away, but he pinned my shoulders.

"Adam, for God's sake, settle down!" cried he. That was impudent, I thought, invoking God, *him*—but then he said, "Don't you understand what you saw? I am a Jew!"

A Jew!

Of course, I had heard of Jews. They lived in the Bible, and in New York City. Their equivocal relationship with Our Savior had won them opprobrium down the ages, and they were not approved of by the Dominion. But I had never seen a living Jew in the flesh—to my knowledge—and I was astonished by the idea that Sam had been one all along: *invisibly*, so to speak.

"You deceived everyone, then!" I said.

"I never claimed to be a Christian! I never spoke of it at all. But what does it matter? You said you had a message from Julian—give it to me, damn you! Where is he?"

I wondered what I should say, or who I might betray if I said it. The world had turned upside-down. All Ben Kreel's lectures on patriotism and fidelity came back to me in one great flood of guilt and shame. Had I been a party to treason as well as atheism?

But I felt I owed this last favor to Julian, who would surely have wanted me to deliver his intelligence whether Sam was a Jew or a Mohammedan: "There are soldiers on all the roads out of town," I said sullenly. "Julian went for Lundsford last night. He says he'll meet you there. Now *get off of me!*"

Sam did so, sitting back on his heels, deep anxiety inscribed upon his face. "Has it begun so soon? I thought they would wait for the New Year."

"I don't know *what* has begun. I don't think I know anything at all!" And, so saying, I leapt to my feet and ran out of the lifeless garden, back to Rapture, who was still tied to the tree where I had left him, nosing unproductively in the undisturbed snow.

I had ridden perhaps an eighth of a mile back toward Williams Ford when another rider came up on my right flank from behind. It was Ben Kreel himself, and he touched his cap and smiled and said, "Do you mind if I ride along with you a ways, Adam Hazzard?"

I could hardly say no.

Ben Kreel was not a pastor—we had plenty of those in Williams Ford, each catering to his own denomination—but he was the head of the local Council of the Dominion of Jesus Christ on Earth, almost as powerful in his way as the men who owned the Estate. And if he was not a pastor, he was at least a sort of shepherd to the townspeople. He had been born right here in Williams Ford, son of a saddler; had been educated, at the Estate's expense, at one of the Dominion Colleges in Colorado Springs; and for the last twenty years he had taught elementary school five days a week and General Christianity on Sundays. I had marked my first letters on a slate board under Ben Kreel's tutelage. Every Independence Day he addressed the townsfolk and reminded them of the symbolism and significance of the Thirteen Stripes and the Sixty Stars; every Christmas, he led the Ecumenical Services at the Dominion Hall.

He was stout and graying at the temples, clean-shaven. He wore a woolen jacket, tall deer hide boots, and a pakool hat not much grander than my own. But he carried himself with an immense dignity, as much in the saddle as on foot. The expression on his face was kindly. It was always kindly. "You're out early, Adam Hazzard," he said. "What are you doing abroad at this hour?"

"Nothing," I said, and blushed. Is there any other word that so spectacularly represents everything it wants to deny? Under the circumstances, "nothing" amounted to a confession of bad intent. "Couldn't sleep," I added hastily. "Thought I might shoot a squirrel or so." That would explain the rifle strapped to my saddle, and it was at least remotely plausible; the squirrels were still active, doing the last of their scrounging before settling in for the cold months.

"On Christmas Eve?" Ben Kreel asked. "And in the copse on the grounds of the Estate? I hope the Duncans and Crowleys don't hear about it. They're jealous of their trees. And I'm sure gunfire would disturb them at this hour. Wealthy men and Easterners prefer to sleep past dawn, as a rule."

"I didn't fire," I muttered. "I thought better of it."

"Well, good. Wisdom prevails. You're headed back to town, I gather?"

"Yes, sir."

"Let me keep you company, then."

"Please do." I could hardly say otherwise, no matter how I longed to be alone with my thoughts.

Our horses moved slowly—the snow made for awkward footing—and Ben Kreel was silent for a long while. Then he said, "You needn't conceal your fears, Adam. I know what's troubling you."

For a moment I had the terrible idea that Ben Kreel had been behind me in the hallway at the Estate, and that he had seen Sam Godwin wrapped in his Old Testament paraphernalia. Wouldn't that create a scandal! (And then I thought that it was exactly such a scandal Sam must have feared all his life: it was worse even than being Church of Signs, for in some states a Jew can be fined or even imprisoned for practicing his faith. I didn't know where Athabaska stood on the issue, but I feared the worst.) But Ben Kreel was talking about conscription, not about Sam.

"I've already discussed this with some of the boys in town," he said. "You're not alone, Adam, if you're wondering what it all means, this military movement, and what might happen as a result of it. And I admit, you're something of a special case. I've been keeping an eye on you. From a distance, as it were. Here, stop a moment."

We had come to a rise in the road, on a bluff above the River Pine, looking south toward Williams Ford from a little height.

"Gaze at that," Ben Kreel said contemplatively. He stretched his arm out in an arc, as if to include not just the cluster of buildings that was the town but the empty fields as well, and the murky flow of the river, and the wheels of the mills, and even the shacks of the indentured laborers down in the low country. The valley seemed at once a living thing, inhaling the crisp atmosphere of the season and breathing out its steams, and a portrait, static in the still blue winter air. As deeply rooted as an oak, as fragile as a ball of Nativity glass.

"Gaze at that," Ben Kreel repeated. "Look at Williams Ford, laid out pretty there. What is it, Adam? More than a place, I think. It's a way of life. It's the sum of all our labors. It's what our fathers have given us and it's what we give our sons. It's where we bury our mothers and where our daughters will be buried."

Here was more Philosophy, then, and after the turmoil of the morning I wasn't sure I wanted any. But Ben Kreel's voice ran on like the soothing syrup my mother used to administer whenever Flaxie or I came down with a cough.

"Every boy in Williams Ford—every boy old enough to submit himself for national service—is just now discovering how reluctant he is to leave the place he knows best. Even you, I suspect."

"I'm no more or less willing than anyone else."

"I'm not questioning your courage or your loyalty. It's just that I know you've had a little taste of what life might be like elsewhere—given how closely you associated yourself with Julian Comstock. Now, I'm sure Julian's a fine young man and an excellent Christian. He could hardly be otherwise, could he, as the nephew of the man who holds this nation in his palm. But his experience has been very different from yours. He's accustomed to cities—to movies like the one we saw at the Hall last night (and I glimpsed you there, didn't I? Sitting in the back pews?)—to books and ideas that might strike a youth of your background as exciting and, well, *different*. Am I wrong?"

"I could hardly say you are, sir."

"And much of what Julian may have described to you is no doubt true. I've traveled some myself, you know. I've seen Colorado Springs, Pittsburgh, even New York City. Our eastern cities are great, proud metropolises—some of the biggest and most productive in the world—and they're worth defending, which is one reason we're trying so hard to drive the Dutch out of Labrador."

"Surely you're right."

"I'm glad you agree. Because there is a trap certain young people fall into. I've seen it before. Sometimes a boy decides that

56

one of those great cities might be a place he can *run away to*—a place where he can escape all the duties, obligations, and moral lessons he learned at his mother's knee. Simple things like faith and patriotism can begin to seem to a young man like burdens, which might be shrugged off when they become too weighty."

"I'm not like that, sir."

"Of course not. But there is yet another element in the calculation. You may have to leave Williams Ford because of the conscription. And the thought that runs through many boys' minds is, if I *must* leave, then perhaps I ought to leave on my own hook, and find my destiny on a city's streets rather than in a battalion of the Athabaska Brigade . . . and you're good to deny it, Adam, but you wouldn't be human if such ideas didn't cross your mind."

"No, sir," I muttered, and I must admit I felt a dawning guilt, for I had in fact been a little seduced by Julian's tales of city life, and Sam's dubious lessons, and the HISTORY OF MANKIND IN SPACE—perhaps I *had* forgotten something of my obligations to the village that lay so still and so inviting in the blue near distance.

"I know," Ben Kreel said, "that things haven't always been easy for your family. Your father's faith, in particular, has been a trial, and we haven't always been good neighbors—speaking on behalf of the village as a whole. Perhaps you've been left out of some activities other boys enjoy as a matter of course: church activities, picnics, common friendships . . . well, even Williams Ford isn't perfect. But I promise you, Adam: if you find yourself in the Brigades, especially if you find yourself tested in time of war, you'll discover that the same boys who shunned you in the dusty streets of your home town become your best friends and bravest defenders, and you theirs. For our common heritage ties us together in ways that may seem obscure, but become obvious under the harsh light of combat."

I had spent so much time smarting under the remarks of other boys (that my father "raised vipers the way other folks raise chickens," for example) that I could hardly credit Ben Kreel's assertion. But I knew little of modern warfare, except what I had read in the novels of Mr. Charles Curtis Easton, so it might be true. And the prospect (as was intended) made me feel even more shame-faced.

"There," Ben Kreel said: "Do you hear that, Adam?"

I did. I could hardly avoid it. The bell was ringing in the Dominion church, calling together one of the early ecumenical services. It was a silvery sound on the winter air, at once lonesome and consoling, and I wanted almost to run toward it—to shelter in it, as if I were a child again.

"They'll want me soon," Ben Kreel said. "Will you excuse me if I ride ahead?"

"No, sir. Please don't mind about me."

"As long as we understand each other, Adam. Don't look so downcast! The future may be brighter than you expect."

"Thank you for saying so, sir."

I stayed a while longer on the low bluff, watching as Ben Kreel's horse carried him toward town. Even in the sunlight it was cold, and I shivered some, perhaps more because of the conflict in my mind than because of the weather. The Dominion man had made me ashamed of myself, and had put into perspective my loose ways of the last few years, and pointed up how many of my native beliefs I had abandoned before the seductive Philosophy of an agnostic young aristo and an aging Jew.

Then I sighed and urged Rapture back along the path toward Williams Ford, meaning to explain to my parents where I had been and reassure them that I would not suffer too much in the coming conscription, to which I would willingly submit.

I was so disheartened by the morning's events that my eyes drifted toward the ground even as Rapture retraced his steps. As I have said, the snows of the night before lay largely undisturbed on this back trail between the town and the Estate. I could see where I had passed this morning, where Rapture's hoofprints were as clearly written as figures in a book. (Ben Kreel must have spent the night at the Estate, and when he left me on the bluff he would have taken the more direct route toward town; only Rapture had passed this way.) Then I reached the place where Julian and I had parted the night before. There were more hoofprints here, in fact a crowd of them—

And I saw something else written (in effect) on the snowy ground—something which alarmed me.

I reined up at once.

I looked south, toward Williams Ford. I looked east, the way Julian had gone the previous night.

Then I took a bracing inhalation of icy air, and followed the trail that seemed to me most urgent.

6

THE EAST-WEST ROAD through Williams Ford is not heavily traveled, especially in winter.

The southern road—also called the "Wire Road," because the telegraph line runs alongside it—connects Williams Ford to the railhead at Connaught, and thus sustains a great deal of traffic. But the east-west road goes essentially nowhere: it is a remnant of a road of the secular ancients, traversed mainly by Tipmen and freelance antiquarians, and then only in the warmer months. I suppose, if you followed the old road as far as it would take you, you might reach the Great Lakes, or somewhere farther east, in that direction; and, the opposite way, you could get yourself lost among washouts and landfalls in the Rocky Mountains. But the railroad—and a parallel turnpike farther south—had obviated the need for all that trouble.

Nevertheless, the east-west road was closely watched where it left the outskirts of Williams Ford. The Reserves had posted a man on a hill overlooking it, the same hill where Julian and Sam and I had paused for blackberries on our way from the Tip last October. But it is a fact that the Reserve troops were held in Reserve, and not sent to the front lines, mainly because of some disabling flaw of body or mind; some were wounded veterans, missing a hand or an arm; some were too simple or sullen to function in a disciplined body of soldiers. I cannot say anything for certain about the man posted as lookout on the hill, but if he was not a fool he was at least utterly unconcerned about concealment, for his silhouette (and that of his rifle) stood etched against the bright eastern sky for all to see. But maybe that was the intent: to let prospective fugitives know their way was barred.

Not *every* way was barred, however, not for someone who had grown up in Williams Ford and hunted everywhere on its perimeter. Instead of following Julian directly I rode north a distance, and then through the crowded lanes of an encampment of indentured laborers (whose ragged children gaped at me from the glassless windows of their shanties, and whose soft-coal fires made a smoky gauze of the motionless air). This route connected with lanes cut through the wheat fields for the transportation of harvests and field-hands—lanes that had been deepened by years of use, so that I rode behind a berm of earth and snake rail fences, hidden from the distant sentinel. When I was safely east, I came down a cattle-trail that reconnected me with the east-west road.

On which I was able to read the same signs that had alerted me back at Williams Ford, thanks to the fine layer of snow still undisturbed by any wind.

Julian had come this way. He had done as he had intended, and ridden toward Lundsford before midnight. The snow had stopped soon thereafter, leaving his horse's hoof-prints clearly visible, though softened and half-covered.

But his were not the only tracks: there was a second set, more crisply defined and hence more recent, probably set down during the night; and this was what I had seen at the crossroads in Williams Ford: evidence of pursuit. Someone had followed Julian, without Julian's knowledge. This had dire implications, the only redeeming circumstance being the fact of a single pursuer rather than a company of men. If the powerful people of the Estate had known that it was Julian Comstock who had fled, they would surely have sent an entire brigade to bring him back. I supposed Julian had been mistaken for a simple miscreant, a labor refugee, or a youngster fleeing the conscription, and that he had been followed by some ambitious Reservist. Otherwise that whole imagined battalion might be right behind me . . . or perhaps soon *would* be, since Julian's absence must have been noted by now.

I rode east, adding my own track to these two.

Before long it was past noon, and I started to have second thoughts as the sun began to angle toward an early rendezvous with the southwestern horizon. What exactly did I hope to accomplish? To warn Julian? If so, I was a little late off the mark . . . though I hoped that at some point Julian had covered his tracks, or otherwise misled his pursuer, who did not have the advantage I had, of knowing where Julian meant to stay until Sam Godwin could arrive. Failing that, I half-imagined *rescuing* Julian from capture, even though I had but a squirrel rifle and a few rounds of ammunition (plus a knife and my own wits, both feeble enough weapons) against whatever a Reservist might carry. In any case these were more wishes and anxieties than calculations or plans; I had no fully-formed plan beyond riding to Julian's aid and telling him that I had delivered my message to Sam, who would be along as soon as he could discreetly leave the Estate.

And then what? It was a question I dared not ask myself—not out on this lonely road, well past the Tip now, farther than I had ever been from Williams Ford; not out here where the flat-lands stretched on each side of the path like the frosty plains of Mars, and the wind, which had been absent all morning, began to pluck at the fringes of my coat, and my shadow elongated in front of me like a scarecrow gone riding. It was cold and get-ting colder, and soon the winter moon would be aloft, and me with only a few ounces of salt pork in my saddlebag and a few matches to make a fire if I was able to secure any kindling by nightfall. I began to wonder if I had gone quite insane. At sev-eral points I thought: I could go back; perhaps I hadn't yet been missed; perhaps it wasn't too late to sit down to a Christmas Eve dinner with my parents, raise a glass of cider to Flaxie and to Christmases past, and wake in time to hear the ring-ing-in of the Holiday and smell the goodness of baked bread and Nativity apples drenched in cinnamon and brown sugar. I mused on it repeatedly, sometimes with tears in my eyes; but I let Rapture continue carrying me toward the darkest part of the horizon.

Then, after what seemed endless hours of dusk, with only a brief pause when both Rapture and I drank from a creek which had a skin of ice on it, I began to come among the ruins of the secular ancients.

Not that there was anything spectacular about them. Fanciful drawings often portray the ruins of the last century as tall buildings, ragged and hollow as broken teeth, forming vine-encrusted canyons and shadowy cul-de-sacs.* No doubt such places exist—most of them in the uninhabitable Southwest, however, where "famine sits enthroned, and waves his scepter over a dominion expressly made for him," which would rule out vines and such tropical items**—but most ruins were like the ones I now passed, mere irregularities (or more precisely, *regularities*) in the landscape, which indicated the former presence of foundations. These terrains were treacherous, often concealing deep basements that could open like hungry mouths on an unwary traveler, and only Tipmen loved them. I was careful to keep to the path, though I began to wonder whether Julian would be as easy to find as I had imagined—"Lundsford" was a big locality, and the wind had already begun to scour away the hoofprints I had relied on for navigation.

I was haunted, too, by thoughts of the False Tribulation of the last century. It was not unusual to come across desiccated human remains in localities like this. Millions had died in the worst dislocations of the End of Oil: of disease, of internecine strife, but mostly of starvation. The Age of Oil had allowed a fierce intensity of fertilization and irrigation of the land, which had fed more people than a humbler agriculture could support. I had seen photographs of Americans from that blighted age, thin as

---

* Or "culs-de-sac"? My French is rudimentary.

** Though Old Miami or Orlando might begin to fit the bill.

sticks, their children with distended bellies, crowded into "relief camps" that would soon enough be transformed into communal graves when the imagined "relief" failed to materialize. No wonder, then, that our ancestors had mistaken those decades for the Tribulation of prophecy. What was astonishing was how many of our current institutions—the Church, the Army, the Federal Government—had survived more or less intact. There was a passage in the Dominion Bible that Ben Kreel had read whenever the subject of the False Tribulation arose in school, and which I had committed to memory: *The field is wasted, the land mourns; for the corn is shriveled, the wine has dried, the oil languishes. Be ashamed, farmers; howl, vinekeepers; howl for the wheat and the barley, for the harvest of the field has perished . . .*

It had made me shiver then, and it made me shiver now, in these barrens which had been stripped of all their utility by a century of scavenging. Where in this rubble was Julian, and where was his pursuer?

It was by his fire I found him. But I was not the first to arrive.

The sun was altogether down, and a hint of the aurora borealis played about the northern sky, dimmed by moonlight, when I came to the most recently excavated section of Lundsford. The temporary dwellings of the Tipmen—rude huts of scavenged timber—had been abandoned here for the season, and corduroy ramps led down into the empty digs.

Here the remnants of last night's snow had been blown into windrows and small dunes, and all evidence of hoofprints had been erased. But I rode slowly, knowing I was close to my destination. I was buoyed by the observation that Julian's pursuer, whoever he was, had not returned this way from his mission: had not, that is, taken Julian captive, or at least had not gone back to Williams Ford with his prisoner in tow. Perhaps the pursuit had been suspended for the night.

It was not long—though it seemed an eternity, as Rapture short-stepped down the frozen road, avoiding snow-hidden pitfalls—before I heard the whickering of another horse, and saw a plume of smoke rising into the moon-bright sky.

Quickly I turned Rapture off the road and tied his reins to the low remnants of a concrete pillar, from which rust-savaged iron rods protruded like skeletal fingers. I took my squirrel rifle from the saddle holster and moved toward the source of the smoke on foot, until I was able to discern that the fumes emerged from a deep declivity in the landscape, perhaps the very dig from which the Tipmen had extracted A HISTORY OF MANKIND IN SPACE. Surely this was where Julian had gone to wait for Sam's arrival. And indeed, here was Julian's horse, one of the finer riding horses from the Estate (worth more, I'm sure, in the eyes of its owner, than a hundred Julian Comstocks), moored to an outcrop . . . and, alarmingly, here was another horse as well, not far away. This second horse was a stranger to me; it was slat-ribbed and elderly-looking; but it wore a military bridle and the sort of cloth bib—blue, with a red star in the middle of it—that marked a mount belonging to the Reserves.

I studied the situation from behind the moon-shadow of a broken abutment.

The smoke suggested that Julian had gone beneath ground, down into the hollow of the Tipmen's dig, to shelter from the cold and bank his fire for the night. The presence of the second horse suggested that he had been discovered, and that his pursuer must already have confronted him.

More than that I could not divine. It remained only to approach the contested grounds as secretively as possible, and see what more I could learn.

I crept closer. The dig was revealed by moonlight as a deep but narrow excavation, covered in part with boards, with a sloping entrance at one end. The glow of the fire within was just visible, as was the chimney-hole that had been cut through the planking some yards farther down. There was, as far as I could discern, only one way in or out. I determined to proceed as far as I could without being seen, and to that end I lowered myself down the slope, inching forward on the seat of my pants over ground that was as cold, it seemed to me, as the wastelands of the Arctic north.

I was slow, I was cautious, and I was quiet. But I was not slow, cautious, or quiet *enough*; for I had just progressed far enough to glimpse an excavated chamber, in which the firelight cast a kaleidoscopic flux of shadows, when I felt a pressure behind my ear—the barrel of a gun—and a voice said, "Keep moving, mister, and join your friend below."

I kept silent until I could comprehend more of the situation I had fallen into.

My captor marched me down into the low part of the dig. The air, if damp, was noticeably warmer here, and we were screened from the increasing wind, though not from the accumulated odors of the fire and the stagnant must of what had once been a basement or cellar in some commercial establishment of the secular ancients.

The Tipmen had not left much behind: only a rubble of broken bits of things, indistinguishable under layers of dust and dirt. The far wall was of concrete, and the fire had been banked against it, under a chimney-hole that must have been cut by the scavengers during their labors. A circle of stones hedged the fire, and the damp planks and splinters in it crackled with a deceptive cheerfulness. Deeper parts of the excavation, with ceilings lower than a man standing erect, opened in several directions.

Julian sat near the fire, his back to the wall and his knees drawn up under his chin. His clothes had been made filthy by the grime of the place. He was frowning, and when he saw me his frown deepened into a scowl.

"Go over there and get beside him," my captor said, "but give me that little bird rifle first."

I surrendered my weapon, modest as it was, and joined Julian. Thus I was able to get my first clear look at the man who had captured me. He appeared not much older than myself, but he was dressed in the blue and yellow uniform of the Reserves. His Reserve cap was pulled low over his eyes, which twitched left and right as though he were in constant fear of an ambush. In short he seemed both inexperienced and nervous—and maybe a little dim, for his jaw was slack, and he was evidently unaware of the dribble of mucous that escaped his nostrils as a result of the cold weather. (But as I have said before, this was not untypical of the members of the Reserve, who were kept out of active duty for a reason.)

His weapon, however, was very much in earnest, and not to be trifled with. It was a Pittsburgh rifle manufactured by the Porter & Earl works, which loaded at the breech from a sort of cassette and could fire five rounds in succession without any more attention from its owner than a twitch of the index finger. Julian had carried a similar weapon but had been disarmed of it; it rested against a stack of small staved barrels, well out of reach, and the Reservist put my squirrel rifle beside it.

I began to feel sorry for myself, and to think what a poor way of spending Christmas Eve I had chosen. I did not resent the action of the Reservist nearly as much as I resented my own stupidity and lapse of judgment.

"I don't know who you are," the Reservist said, "and I don't care—one draft-dodger is as good as the next, in my opinion— but I was given the job of collecting runaways, and my bag is getting full. I hope you'll both keep till morning, when I can ride you back into Williams Ford. Anyhow, none of us shall sleep tonight. I won't, in any case, so you might as well resign yourself to your captivity. If you're hungry, there's a little meat."

I was never less hungry in my life, and I began to say so, but Julian interrupted: "It's true, Adam," he said, "we're fairly caught. I wish you hadn't come after me."

"I'm beginning to feel the same way," I said.

He gave me a meaningful look, and said in a lower voice, "Is Sam—?"

"No whispering there," our captor said at once.

But I divined the intent of the question, and nodded to indi-
cate that I had delivered Julian's message, though that was by no
means a guarantee of our deliverance. Not only were the exits
from Williams Ford under close watch, but Sam could not slip
away as inconspicuously as I had, and if Julian's absence had
been noted there would have been a redoubling of the guard,
and perhaps an expedition sent out to hunt us. The man who had
captured Julian was evidently an outrider, assigned to patrol the
roads for runaways, and he had been diligent in his work.

He was somewhat less diligent now that he had us in his
control, however, for he took a wooden pipe from his pocket,
and proceeded to fill it, as he made himself as comfortable as
possible on a wooden crate. His gestures were still nervous, and I
supposed the pipe was meant to relax him; for it was not tobacco
he put into it.

The Reservist might have been a Kentuckian, for I understand
the less respectable people of that State often form the habit of
smoking the silk of the female hemp plant, which is cultivated
prodigiously there. Kentucky hemp is grown for cordage and
cloth and paper, and as a drug is less intoxicating than the Indian
Hemp of lore; but its mild smoke is said to be pleasant for those
who indulge in it, though too much can result in sleepiness and
great thirst.

Julian evidently thought these symptoms would be welcome
distractions in our captor, and he gestured to me to remain silent,
so as not to interrupt the Reservist in his vice. The Reservist
packed the pipe's bowl with dried vegetable matter from an
oilcloth envelope he carried in his pocket, and soon the sub-

stance was alight, and a slightly more fragrant smoke joined the effluvium of the camp-fire as it swirled toward the rent in the ceiling.

Clearly the night would be a long one, and I tried to be patient in my captivity, and not think too much of Christmas matters, or the yellow light of my parents' cottage on dark winter mornings, or the soft bed where I might have been sleeping if I had not been rash in my deliberations.

7

I BEGAN BY SAYING this was a story about Julian Comstock, and I fear I lied, for it has turned out mainly to be a story about myself.

But there is a reason for this, beyond the obvious temptations of vanity and self-regard. I did not at the time know Julian nearly as well as I thought I did.

Our friendship was essentially a boys' friendship. I could not help reviewing, as we sat in silent captivity in the ruins of Lundsford, the things we had done together: reading books, hunting in the wooded foothills west of Williams Ford, arguing amiably over everything from Philosophy and Moon-Visiting to the best way to bait a hook or cinch a bridle. It had been too easy, during our time together, to forget that Julian was an aristo with close connections to men of power, or that his father had been famous both as a hero and as a traitor, or that his uncle Deklan Comstock, the President, might not have Julian's best interests at heart.

All that seemed far away, and distant from the nature of Julian's true spirit, which was gentle and inquisitive—a naturalist's disposition, not a politician's or a general's. When I pictured Julian as an adult, I imagined him contentedly pursuing some scholarly or artistic adventure: digging the bones of pre-Noachian monsters out of the Athabaska shale, perhaps, or making an improved kind of movie. He was not a warlike person, and the thoughts of the great men of the day seemed almost exclusively concerned with war.

So I had let myself forget that he was *also* everything he had been before he came to Williams Ford. He was the heir of a brave, determined, and ultimately betrayed father, who had conquered an army of Brazilians but had been crushed by the millstone of political intrigue. He was the son of a powerful woman, born to a powerful family of her own—not powerful enough to save Bryce Comstock from the gallows, but powerful enough to protect Julian, at least temporarily, from the mad calculations of his uncle. He was both a pawn and a player in the great games of the aristos. And while I had forgotten all this, Julian had *not*—these were the people who had made him, and if he chose not to speak of them, they nevertheless must have haunted his thoughts.

He was, it is true, often frightened of small things—I still remember his disquiet when I described the rituals of the Church of Signs to him, and he would sometimes shriek at the distress of animals when our hunting failed to result in a clean kill. But tonight, here in the ruins, I was the one who half-dozed in a morose funk, fighting tears; while it was Julian who sat intently still, gazing with resolve from beneath the strands of dusty hair that straggled over his brows, as coolly calculating as a bank clerk.

When we hunted, he often gave me the rifle to fire the last lethal shot, distrusting his own resolve.

Tonight—had the opportunity presented itself—I would have given the rifle to him.

I half-dozed, as I said, and from time to time woke to see the Reservist still sitting in guard. His eyelids were at half-mast, but I put that down to the effect of the hemp flowers he had smoked. Periodically he would start, as if at a sound inaudible to others, then settle back into place.

He had boiled a copious amount of coffee in a tin pan, and he warmed it whenever he renewed the fire, and drank sufficiently to keep him from falling asleep. Of necessity, this meant he must once in a while retreat to a distant part of the dig and attend to physical necessities in relative privacy. This did not give us any advantage, however, since he carried his Pittsburgh rifle with him, but it allowed a moment or two in which Julian could whisper without being overheard.

"This man is no mental giant," Julian said. "We may yet get out of here with our freedom."

"It's not his *brains* so much as his *artillery* that's stopping us," said I.

"Perhaps we can separate the one from the other. Look there, Adam. Beyond the fire—back in the rubble."

I looked.

There was motion in the shadows, which I began to recognize.

"The distraction may suit our purposes," Julian said, "unless it becomes fatal." And I saw the sweat that had begun to stand out on his forehead, the terror barely hidden in his eyes. "But I need your help."

I have said that I did not take part in the particular rites of my father's church, and that snakes were not my favorite creatures. This is true. As much as I have heard about surrendering one's volition to God—and I had seen my father with a Massassauga Rattler in each hand, trembling with devotion, speaking in a tongue not only foreign but utterly unknown (though it favored long vowels and stuttered consonants, much like the sounds he made when he burned his fingers on the coal stove)—I could never entirely assure myself that I would be protected by divine will from the serpent's bite. Some in the congregation obviously had not been: there was Sarah Prestley, for instance, whose right arm had swollen up black with venom and had to be amputated by Williams Ford's physician . . . but I will not dwell on that. The point is, that while I *disliked* snakes, I was not especially *afraid* of them, as Julian was. And I could not help admiring his restraint: for what was writhing in the shadows nearby was a nest of snakes that had been aroused by the heat of the fire.

I should add that it was not uncommon for these collapsed ruins to be infested with snakes, mice, spiders, and poisonous insects. Death by bite or sting was one of the hazards routinely faced by Tipmen, the others including concussion, blood poisoning, and accidental burial. The snakes, after the Tipmen ceased work for the winter, must have crept into this chasm anticipating an undisturbed hibernation, of which we and the Reservist had unfortunately deprived them.

The Reservist—who came back a little unsteadily from his necessaries—had not yet noticed these prior tenants. He seated himself on his crate, scowled at us, and studiously refilled his pipe.

"If he discharges all five shots from his rifle," Julian whispered, "then we have a chance of overcoming him, or of recovering our own weapons. But, Adam—"

"No talking there," the Reservist mumbled.

"—*you must remember your father's advice,*" Julian finished.

"I said keep quiet!"

Julian cleared his throat and addressed the Reservist directly, since the time for action had obviously arrived: "Sir, I have to draw your attention to something."

"What would that be, my little draft dodger?"

"I'm afraid we're not alone in this terrible place."

"Not alone!" the Reservist said, casting his eyes about him nervously. Then he recovered and squinted at Julian. "I don't see any other persons."

"I don't mean persons, but vipers," said Julian.

"Vipers!"

"In other words—snakes."

At this the Reservist started again, his mind perhaps still slightly confused by the effects of the hemp smoke; then he sneered and said, "Go on, you can't pull that one on me."

"I'm sorry if you think I'm joking, for there are at least a dozen snakes advancing from the shadows, and one of them is about to achieve intimacy with your right boot."*

"Hah," the Reservist said, but he could not help glancing in the indicated direction, where one of the serpents—a fat and

---

* Julian's sense of timing was exquisite, perhaps as a result of his theatrical inclinations.

lengthy example—had indeed lifted its head and was sampling the air above his bootlace.

The effect was immediate, and left no more time for planning. The Reservist leapt from his seat on the wooden crate, uttering oaths, and danced backward, at the same time attempting to bring his rifle to his shoulder and confront the threat. He discovered to his dismay that it was not a question of *one* snake but of *dozens*, and he compressed the trigger of the weapon reflexively. The resulting shot went wild. The bullet impacted near the main nest of the creatures, causing them to scatter with astonishing speed, like a box of loaded springs—unfortunately for the hapless Reservist, who was directly in their path. He cursed vigorously and fired four more times. Some of the shots careened harmlessly; at least one obliterated the midsection of the lead serpent, which knotted around its own wound like a bloody rope.

"Now, Adam!" Julian shouted, and I stood up, thinking: My father's advice?

My father was a taciturn man, and most of his advice had involved the practical matter of running the Estate's stables. I hesitated a moment in confusion, while Julian advanced toward the captive rifles, dancing among the surviving snakes like a dervish. The Reservist, recovering somewhat, raced in the same direction; and then I recalled the only advice of my father's that I had ever shared with Julian:

Grasp it where its neck ought to be, behind the head; ignore the tail, however it may thrash; and crack its skull, hard and often enough to subdue it.

And so I did just that—until the threat was neutralized.

Julian, meanwhile, recovered the weapons, and came away from the infested area of the dig.

He looked with some astonishment at the Reservist, who was slumped at my feet, bleeding from his scalp, which I had "cracked, hard and often."

"Adam," he said. "When I spoke of your father's advice—I meant the *snakes*."

"The snakes?" Several of them still twined about the dig. But I reminded myself that Julian knew very little about the nature and variety of reptiles. "They're only corn snakes," I explained.* "They're big, but they're not venomous."

Julian, his eyes gone large, absorbed this information.

Then he looked at the crumpled form of the Reservist again.

"Have you killed him?"

"Well, I hope not," I said.

---

* Once confined to the southeast, corn snakes have spread north with the warming climate. I have read that certain of the secular ancients used to keep them as pets—yet another instance of our ancestors' willful perversity.

8

WE MADE A NEW CAMP, in a less populated part of the ruins, and kept a watch on the road, and at dawn we saw a single horse and rider approaching from the west. It was Sam Godwin.

Julian hailed him, waving his arms. Sam came closer, and looked with some relief at Julian, and then speculatively at me. I blushed, thinking of how I had interrupted him at his prayers (however unorthodox those prayers might have been, from a purely Christian perspective), and how poorly I had reacted to my discovery of his true religion. But I said nothing, and Sam said nothing, and relations between us seemed to have been regularized, since I had demonstrated my loyalty (or foolishness) by riding to Julian's aid.

It was Christmas morning. I supposed that did not mean anything in particular to Julian or Sam, but I was poignantly aware of the date. The sky was blue again, but a squall had passed during the dark hours of the morning, and the snow "lay round about, deep and crisp and even." Even the ruins of Lundsford were transformed into something soft-edged and oddly beautiful. I was amazed at how simple it was for nature to cloak corruption in the garb of purity and make it peaceful.

But it would not be peaceful for long, and Sam said so. "There are troops behind me as we speak. Word came by wire from New York not to let Julian escape. We can't linger here more than a moment."

"Where will we go?" Julian asked.

"It's impossible to ride much farther east. There's no forage for the animals and precious little water. Sooner or later we'll have to turn south and make a connection with the railroad or the turnpike. It's going to be short rations and hard riding for a while, I'm afraid, and if we do make good our escape we'll have to assume new identities. We'll be little better than draft dodgers or labor refugees, and I expect we'll have to pass some time among that hard crew, at least until we reach New York City. We can find friends in New York."

It was a plan, but it was a large and lonesome one, and my heart sank at the prospect.

"We have a prisoner," Julian told his mentor, and he took Sam back into the excavated ruins to explain how we had spent the night.

The Reservist was there, hands tied behind his back, a little groggy from the punishment I had inflicted on him but well enough to open his eyes and scowl. Julian and Sam spent a little time debating how to deal with this encumbrance. We could not, of course, take him with us; the question was how to return him to his superiors without endangering ourselves unnecessarily.

It was a debate to which I could contribute nothing, so I took a little slip of paper from my back-satchel, and a pencil, and wrote a letter.

It was addressed to my mother, since my father was without the art of literacy.

You will no doubt have noticed my absence, I wrote. *It saddens me to be away from home, especially at this time (I write on Christmas Day). But I hope you will be consoled with the knowledge that I am all right, and not in any immediate danger.*

(This was a lie, depending on how you defined "immediate," but a kindly one, I reasoned.)

In any case I would not have been able to remain in Williams Ford, since I could not have escaped the draft for long even if I postponed my military service for some few more months. The conscription drive is in earnest; the War in Labrador must be going badly. It was inevitable that we should be separated, as much as I yearn for my home and all its comforts.

(And it was all I could do not to decorate the page with a vagrant tear.)

Please accept my best wishes and my gratitude for everything you and Father have done for me. I will write again as soon as is practicable, which may not be immediately. Trust in the knowledge that I will pursue my destiny faithfully and with every Christian virtue you have taught me. God bless you in the coming and every year.

That was not enough to say, but there wasn't time for more. Julian and Sam were calling for me. I signed my name, and added, as a postscript:

Please tell Father that I value his advice, and that it has already served me usefully. Yrs. etc. once again, Adam.

"You've written a letter," Sam observed as he came to rush me to my horse. "But have you given any thought to how you might mail it?"

I confessed that I had not.

"The Reservist can carry it," said Julian, who had already mounted his horse.

The Reservist was also mounted, but with his hands tied behind him, as it was Sam's final conclusion that we should set him loose with the horse headed west, where he would encounter more troops before very long. He was awake but, as I have said, sullen; and he barked, "I'm nobody's damned mailman!"

I addressed the message, and Julian took it and tucked it into the Reservist's saddlebag. Despite his youth, and despite the slightly dilapidated condition of his hair and clothing, Julian sat tall in the saddle. I had never thought of him as high-born until that moment, when an aspect of command seemed to enter his body and his voice. He said to the Reservist, "We treated you kindly—"

The Reservist uttered an oath.

"Be quiet. You were injured in the conflict, but we took you prisoner, and we've treated you in a more gentlemanly fashion than we were when the conditions were reversed. I am a Comstock—at least for the moment—and I won't be spoken to crudely by an infantryman, at any price. You'll deliver this boy's message, and you'll do it gratefully."

The Reservist was clearly awed by the assertion that Julian was a Comstock—he had been laboring under the assumption that we were mere village runaways—but he screwed up his courage and said, "Why should I?"

"Because it's the Christian thing to do," Julian said, "and if this argument with my uncle is ever settled, the power to remove your head from your shoulders may well reside in my hands. Does that make sense to you, soldier?"

The Reservist allowed that it did.

And so we rode out that Christmas morning from the ruins in which the Tipmen had discovered the HISTORY OF MANKIND IN SPACE, which still resided in my back-satchel, vagrant memory of a half-forgotten past.

My mind was a confusion of ideas and anxieties, but I found myself recalling what Julian had said, long ago it now seemed, about DNA, and how it aspired to perfect replication but progressed by remembering itself imperfectly. It might be true, I thought, because our lives were like that—*time itself* was like that, every moment dying and pregnant with its own distorted reflection. Today was Christmas: which Julian claimed had once been a pagan holiday, dedicated to Sol Invictus or some other Roman god; but which had evolved into the familiar celebration of the present, and was no less dear because of it.

(I imagined I could hear the Christmas bells ringing from the Dominion Hall at Williams Ford, though that was impossible, for we were miles away, and not even the sound of a cannon shot could carry so far across the prairie. It was only memory speaking.)

And maybe this logic was true of people, too; maybe I was already becoming an inexact echo of what I had been just days before. Maybe the same was true of Julian. Already something hard and uncompromising had begun to emerge from his gentle features—the first manifestation of a new Julian, a freshly *evolved* Julian, called forth by his violent departure from Williams Ford, or slouching toward New York to be born.

But that was all Philosophy, and not much use, and I kept quiet about it as we spurred our horses in the direction of the railroad, toward the rude and squalling infant Future.